AMERICAN CLOCKS

Other Main Street Pocket Guides

Available Now

The Main Street Pocket Guide to Quilts
The Main Street Pocket Guide to Dolls
The Main Street Pocket Guide to American Longarms

Forthcoming

The Main Street Pocket Guide to American Pottery & Porcelain
The Main Street Pocket Guide to Pressed Glass
The Main Street Pocket Guide to American Toys
The Main Street Pocket Guide to American Silver and Silver Plate

The Main Street Pocket Guide to

AMERICAN CLOCKS

ANITA SCHORSCH

The Main Street Press

Pittstown, New Jersey

Copyright© 1981 by The Main Street Press

First Main Street edition, 1983

The Main Street Press
William Case House
Pittstown, New Jersey 08867

Printed in the United States of America

Library of Congress Cataloging in Publication Data

Schorsch, Anita.
  The Main Street pocket guide to American clocks.

  Bibliography: p. 252
  Includes index.
  1. Clocks and watches—United States—Collectors and collecting.
I. Title. II. Title: Pocket guide to American clocks.
NK7484.S36   1983   681.1'13'0973   83-61592
ISBN 0-915590-37-9

Contents

How to Use This Book

The purpose of this book is to provide the collector with a visual identification guide to American timekeepers. To this end, an attempt has been made to classify clocks and timepieces (excluding watches) according to the stylistic position that their cases occupy in the decorative arts and to look at them in sympathy with their periods of origin and stylistic influences. This visual guide, then, classifies the American clock **from the outside in** and acknowledges the fact, right or wrong, that most people who buy antique clocks are responding essentially to the case that houses a movement rather than to the movement that happens to be housed within the case.

The broadest possible way to classify timekeepers, of course, is by **placement**—that is, where is the clock placed: on the floor, on the wall, on a shelf, a table, a mantel? For this reason, the book consists of three basic categories—Tall Case (or Floor) Clocks, Wall Clocks, and Shelf Clocks—all of which, in turn, are subdivided into major classifications of their own. These classifications, fifty in all, have been determined by the **clearly visible characteristics** of the case, characteristics that almost any collector will be able to recognize through perusing the illustrations in this book.

Suppose you spot an unidentified clock that appeals to you at a flea market or in an antiques shop. Perhaps the dealer has told you the obvious: "It is a Victorian mantel clock." But there are thousands of so-called Victorian mantel clocks. Exactly what kind of mantel clock is it? And when was it made? By turning to the Color Key (pp. 17-48), you will find among the fifty color illustrations a photograph of a clock that bears a close "family resemblance" to the one you're interested in—the visible characteristics, the basic shape, are definitely similar. Under the color illustration will be found the name of the classification and the page numbers in the guide that discuss and illustrate clocks in that category. By turning to these pages, you will be able to find the identical clock that you are interested in (or clocks similar to it), and you will discover, among other things, its approximate date of manufacture, its maker, its type of movement, its composition, its stylistic origins, and its approximate value.

Using this guide, then, is very simple. To repeat: once you find a clock that you want to find out more about, turn to the Color Key (pp. 17-48), find the color photograph that most closely identifies the classification of your clock, and turn to the pages indicated for further information.

Each of the 500 clocks discussed in this guide is treated in a separate numbered entry, containing basic information. A typical entry is reproduced on p. 9, together with a list of all the elements contained in each entry of the book, from date and maker to movement and price. Most of these elements are self-explanatory. But two require a word of introduction.

Clock or Timepiece: Each timekeeper has been designated a clock or a timepiece according to whether or not it has a striking train. This fact can generally be observed by noting the number of wind squares or arbors visible on the dial. In general, if a timekeeper has one wind square, it is a timepiece; if it has two, it is a clock. But there are exceptions. A second wind square on a true Regulator dial indicates two power sources for the single time train. Conversely, a clock without any wind squares may have a striking train which is wound instead by pull-up weights.

Price Range: This is a treacherous area, so let no one fool you into thinking that any so-called price guide is a completely accurate means of determining a clock's value. Essentially, a clock is worth whatever a collector is willing to pay for it. Still, there have to be guidelines, and this guide offers not prices, per se, but **price ranges** based on the following considerations: (1) that the clock is in good condition; that is, with minor restoration as defined by recognized experts; (2) that the movement is original to the case. The price ranges suggested in this guide are coded as follows:

A — $15,000 and over
B — $7,000 to $15,000
C — $5,000 to $7,500
D — $1,000 to $5,000
E — $500 to $1,000
F — $100 to $500
G — Below $100

Please note that the prices given are not necessarily for the specific clock illustrated, but are suggestive of the **type** of clock pictured. Two clocks of the same model, for example, may vary in worth because of condition and the number of replacement parts in each.

Although this guide deals specifically with American clocks, there are three exceptions that should be noted: (1) the English lantern clock (section 3) is included because it was the first timekeeper used in the early American home; (2) the French figured mantel clock honoring George Washington (42-1, 42-2), designed sixty years before the American figured mantel, is included because it was made expressly for the American market; (3) a few European-American schoolhouse (12-8), round-top (37-1) and porcelain clocks (34-3) are included because their movements were made by American manufacturers.

A Typical Entry

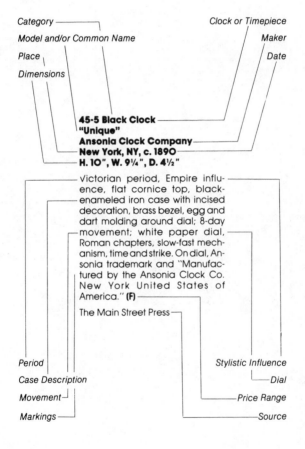

Category

Model and/or Common Name

Place

Dimensions

Clock or Timepiece

Maker

Date

45-5 Black Clock
"Unique"
Ansonia Clock Company
New York, NY, c. 1890
H. 10", W. 9¼", D. 4½"

Victorian period, Empire influence, flat cornice top, black-enameled iron case with incised decoration, brass bezel, egg and dart molding around dial; 8-day movement; white paper dial, Roman chapters, slow-fast mechanism, time and strike. On dial, Ansonia trademark and "Manufactured by the Ansonia Clock Co. New York United States of America." **(F)**

The Main Street Press

Period

Case Description

Movement

Markings

Stylistic Influence

Dial

Price Range

Source

Introduction

Among the earliest colonizers of America were gentlemen, ministers, and enterprising sea captains who, though they did not themselves tinker with balance wheels, weights, springs, and clock pendulums, did bring over a few clocks among their prized possessions. Records show that colonist Henry Packs brought a small brass lantern clock to America which he later bequeathed to a Hartford church. Other early settlers also brought with them hanging lantern clocks, although they might have carried instead the tall weight-driven movement without a case dubbed today a "hang-up" or "wag-on-the-wall." One further possibility was the portable, expensive, and inaccurate spring-driven shelf or table clock, misnamed "bracket clock," a form American genius would bring to fruition in the nineteenth century and successfully export back to the Old World.

Who were the first American clockmakers, and what were their trades? Although the Dutch in the Old World were credited with the first pendulum-driven timekeepers, and the Germans had perfected the table variety and the wooden movement wag-on-the-wall, the first professional clockmakers to appear publicly in the colonies were two Englishmen advertising in the **Boston News Letter**. In 1707 and in 1708 James Batterson and Isaac Webb each ran separate ads offering to do the same job—to make any kind of clock that a person could desire or turn any kind of clock into the new pendulum variety. The ads suggest that these early clockmakers understood contemporary brass movements and were aware of the new pendulum styles. Like other early clock artisans, excepting the Germans of the Black Forest, American clockmakers were men of the metal trades—locksmiths, gunsmiths, blacksmiths, silversmiths, or jewelers. An interest in clock cases and a pocketbook to afford them soon encouraged men of the wooden trades—carpenters, joiners, cabinetmakers, and carvers—to work in the clock trade. As early as 1712 the well-to-do of Boston bought Benjamin Bagnall's clocks "in hard wood cases." At the end of the century when cheaper clock movements were successfully made out of wood, the craft of the carpenter was of invaluable assistance. Families like the Dominys of East Hampton, New York, combined the multiple skills of clockmaking, cabinetmaking, house building, wheelwrighting, toolmaking, gunsmithing and metalworking. By the beginning of the nineteenth century, however, the manufacturer-merchant—the man who organized, assembled, and distributed the goods—considered himself the clockmaker and put his name on the dial, and assuredly on the bill.

The brass-movement wooden tall-case clock was the earliest and most popular form of timekeeper made in America through 1790. Resembling other pieces of case furniture, the first clock cases included a flat top (or a "square head") or a sarcophagus or step top. In 1740 during the so-called Queen Anne period it was fashionable to find the head rounded like a dome. By the 1750s an "Arch'd head and scrolled pediment" of the so-called Chippendale and later Federal period appeared, the Federal scroll sometimes described as an elongated or "swan-neck." It was not unusual to find the line and form of the four eighteenth-century head styles being repeated in the Victorian era with minor alterations in proportion, woods, and surface design.

The buyers, and there were few of them until after the Revolution, reasonably preferred clocks which contained the latest and most sophisticated mechanisms—long-running movements, second hands, alarms, calendars, repeaters, and ages or phases of the moon. But more buyers also found themselves looking for a decorative object "in the newest taste," following the fashionable line in case furniture set by the cabinetmakers of London. Rural cabinetmakers, also concerned with the newest taste, often simulated in paint the fine graining they observed on the mahogany or walnut high-style city clocks, and though they were not always able to carve the rosettes and fretwork that ornamented the stylish clock heads, they provided provincial "whale's tails" or solid cresting—the country or vernacular touch of the so-called Chippendale high style.

By the last decade of the eighteenth century the heavy, robust case had become old fashioned. The tall-case clock now developed slender proportions in line with the new classical or Federal taste revived by the French, copied in English pattern books by George Hepplewhite (1788), Thomas Sheraton (1791), and Thomas Hope (1801), and reinterpreted by the keen eye of American clockcase makers catering to what many believe was a distinct American taste. The architectural scrolls of the broken arch became attenuated; the rosettes dwindled into smaller, flatter flowers; the curve of the ogee bracket feet straightened. Painted surfaces and wood inlay replaced ornamental carving and raised panels. And underlying the new slim, flat, ascetic design was a conservative yearning in Americans to be reunited with the cultural past. Artisans adopted antiquity's allegorical symbols of universal truth and beauty—bell flowers, wheat husks, eagles, laurel wreaths, grape vines, conch shells, lyres, urns, and languishing female figures—to echo America's political and religious independence and yet tie her to a great cultural and eclectic past.

The clocks which best carried the new ornamental message to a burgeoning group of comfortable people were not the tall clocks, but the smaller, relatively less expensive brass or wood-movement wall and shelf timekeeps like the banjo, the girandole, the pillar and scroll, and the column. They were portable, high style, and remarkably accurate—quite as precise as the tall-case movements with spring, escapement, and pendulum improvements. The production of shelf and hanging clocks catapulted with the mechanical and artistic brilliance of the Willard family, the innovative mechanics of the Terry family, and the master merchandising of the Jerome family. Such practical "Yankee ingenuity," foretold by American poetess Martha Brewster in 1758 as the trait that would bring America into her "age of bloom," characterized the entire period following the War of 1812. With moveable circular saws, planing machines, ogee cutters, fine veneers, and sandpaper wheels to make their stylish cases, and the coiled brass springs, "rolling pinions," and brass in sheets to make their improved movements, the business of making clocks took on grand proportions. The Patent Office records of the period demonstrate that it was an age in which inventive genius was more spectacular than in any other period of recorded history.

The Revolutionary War and the War of 1812 had limited foreign trade and encouraged local craftsmen and manufacturers, particularly those from rural areas and those from places like Connecticut where the non-importation acts had been enforced from the beginning of the revolutionary period. These men had more working for them, however, than a military economy. They had an inherent commitment, drawn from their own conservative, small-town, revivalist backgrounds which propelled them to work and helped them to sell. Mass production was viewed by them as a benevolent gesture, the control of time and the precision of timekeepers as a social good. Henry Terry, looking back, credited God with having given Connecticut clockmakers special powers of "industry, enterprise, and skill." Like Terry, clockmakers functioned believing that they were part of a great civilizing movement.

With the union of the craftsman and the machine in the nineteenth century, men were both freer and more able to explore their own eclectic tastes and reproduce easily what they admired from the past. Carved rococo design reappeared in the Victorian iron, porcelain, and papier-mâché clock cases. Makers like Asa Munger, Joseph Ives, Heman Clark, Seth Thomas, Silas Hoadley, Olcott Cheney, Luman Watson, Lemuel Curtis, and Hiram Camp chose classical Greek, Roman, and Egyptian motifs revived by the French —eagles, gilt columns, and paw feet—which they easily found in the new English pattern books of George Smith (1826), T. King (1830s), Andrew J. Downing (1850), and Blackie and Son (1853). Clockmakers and peddlers saw to it that for every farmer "in Kentucky, Indiana, Illinois, Missouri, and . . . in every dell of Arkansas . . . [and for] every cabin where there was not a chair to sit on there was sure to be a Connecticut clock." Some semblance of the Greek architectural order, if only in columns, ogee curves, or anthemion leaves, was everywhere. At least this was the report of English scientist G.W. Featherstonbaugh after traveling through America in the 1840s.

By 1850 most people were purchasing more than a mere mechanical timekeeper; they acquired clocks because of the cultural, patriotic, or social values associated with the design of the case. Technical standards of the cabinetmaking trade which distinguished objects made by hand from those made by machine had been dropped and no critical, historical, or social objections were voiced until the late-Victorian period when the writings of John Ruskin and William Morris were circulated in America. Fighting the effects of another revolution—this time the one created by industry —Ruskin, Morris, and finally the various proponents of the Arts and Crafts Movement openly opposed mass production, production for profit, and the "command over nature, and greater hurry of life." They condemned the workman no longer a craftsman, the factory no longer a shop, and clocks no longer a product of art begun and finished by the same man.

But the machine had existed long before the so-called "modern age," just as interchangeable parts and special parts makers had also existed in earlier periods. The clock, like other pieces of furniture, had always been both handcrafted and manufactured, and as Henry Terry, son of the great Eli Terry, explained it in **American Clock Making** (1870), the engine which cut the gear wheels, and the presses, the lathe, and the variety of drills, were all machines whether driven by hand, by foot, or even by steam. And they too represented the process we still call today "Made by Hand."

Since this guide is divided into three primary parts—tall-case clocks, wall clocks, and shelf clocks—some historical background for each is relevant here.

Tall Case Clocks

Although the deferential phrase "grandfather's clock" has been used since it first appeared in 1875 following the popular song by the same name, the tall-case clock was indiscriminately referred to in eighteenth-century inventories, account books, and newspaper ads as a "New Clock" (a clock with a pendulum, then a new invention), a "newly Fashion'd Monethly Clock and Case," and "a fine House Clock." Only rarely, as in an ad in 1742 for a "Standing Clock" or in a 1748 ad for a repeating or plain clock with or without a case, was the tall clock distinguished from a lantern, bracket, or table model. The long pendulum clock with power coming from its hanging weights, was not then, as it is now, a family heirloom or cultural artifact. It was a modern, expensive, mechanical, contrivance which served a very specific purpose: telling the time.

By 1750 the tall case as a piece of furniture was attracting the attention of prominent Americans. And with good reason. Such mirrors of taste as **Universal Magazine** were calling the latest Chippendale cases" the genteelest Piece of Furniture" a man could own. By the 1770s urban clock and case makers, like Philadelphian David Evans, were trying to reach the moderate buyer, as well as the elite, the man living in as well as out of the city, the one who wanted a case "in the neatest manner, and newest fashion and at the lowest prices." Benjamin Willard, brother of the famous "banjo" clockmaker Simon, sold tall clocks cheaper than could be gotten in London, with the guarantee that they were still made "in the best Manner." He advertised that his cases were made in the same shop as his movements and that he delivered to any part of the country.

The average tall-case clock made in the first half of the eighteenth century generally cost between £3 and £9. During the remainder of the century, with such exceptions as the 1780s when paper currency had become almost valueless, a tall clock could usually be bought for between £6 and £30. The late-eighteenth-century shop records of Daniel Burnap of Connecticut show that buyers frequently bartered rather than paid for the clocks they ordered. "A Hors Waggon compleet" and fifty dollars in cash paid for a Burnap tall clock which must have resembled the fine brass-wheeled chime clock with a case which Burnap sold for £30 or $100. (Burnap's $100 was equal to what about $2500 would buy today.

The fourth quarter of the century brought back to favor an old and rural-style wooden movement inspired by the original German Black Forest clocks of the seventeenth century. By replacing the brass wheels with wooden ones, and the brass dials with paper and painted wooden dials, clockmakers could accommodate their clocks to the shortage of brass caused by the American Revolution. Although the adaptations reduced the costs of the tall-case clock, nothing kept it from disappearing under a wave of "New Fashioned" shelf clocks and wall hanging masterpieces. It was three-quarters of a century before antiquarian pursuits would revive the tall-clock form, before idealistic writers would sentimentalize the hand-craftsmanship they remembered in the big clocks, before the nation's Centennial would infuse the spirit of patriotism and the glory of the American family into the grandfather timekeeper, making of it a national icon. Upon this stately clock form was imposed a nostalgia for the American past, for national "roots," that has superseded function in almost every tall-case clock built since the Centennial.

Wall Clocks

Although the tall clock was the first timekeeper crafted in the American colonies, the wall clock was the first timekeeper to reflect to the fullest the new Federal style. Following the English brass lantern clock, which was the original domestic hanging timekeeper for the entire Anglo-American world, Americans developed their own elegant small-case, small-movement, hanging timekeeper, commonly called today a Massachusetts wall clock. Though it had limited production, its movement was the basis for the "patent timepiece," later called a banjo—a light-weight eight-day accurate-movement timekeeper which contributed a novel shape and proportion to the American interior. With the new painted and gilt look in glass and wood, with geometric and sometimes patriotic motifs to suit national pride, it satisfied American fantasies of luxury and refinement at a third the size and a third the price of an average tall clock. Production, however, lagged until the middle of the nineteenth century. This understated but "Improved Timepiece," as its creator Simon Willard called it, inspired further creative interpretations—the diamond head, the girandole, and the lyre—by other New Englanders like Lemuel Curtis, Daniel Munroe, Jabez Baldwin, and J.G. Brown.

Since accuracy was still a high priority in the increasingly industrial commonwealth, wall chronometers, marine and astronomical timepieces, and regulators appeared on the walls of clockmakers' and jewelers' shops next to the more simple timekeepers aimed for domestic use. The regulator was a precision clock made with a mercury-compensation, gridiron, or alloy pendulum and was useful to jewelers, watchmen, and railroad controllers who needed accurate time measurers to improve their own efficiency. A long hanging case similar to the eighteenth-century English "act of Parliament" or "inn" clock evoked a feeling of quality which remained associated with the long drop even when nineteenth-century manufacturers reproduced the shape and name "Regulator" across the glass without supplying the high-quality movement associated with it. When the drop design was shortened, the case form became known as the "schoolhouse" clock.

As the century progressed, innovations were added to the wall clock—indeed to all clocks—which were not necessarily related to the clock mechanism itself. For example, artisans from Connecticut and New Hampshire as well as from New York and Massachusetts produced a looking-glass timekeeper, permitting two functions from one device. Not only could the modern American conveniently tell time, but he could shave, comb his hair, or read by the mirror's reflected light. Although Joseph Ives and probably Aaron Willard before him were among the first to produce the wall mirror clock,

Chauncey Jerome's "bronze looking-glass" shelf variation which followed is still the mirror timekeeper most prized by collectors today.

Inevitably, most of the fashionable wall clocks were replaced by cheaper shelf clocks, and catalogues after the 1850s advertised many inexpensive examples. But the same energy and organization which produced the cheap clock also continued to produce the fine clock, and one obvious key to the identification of a quality movement is the price tag which over the centuries has never lessened.

Shelf Clocks

The American shelf clock began in the Federal period with the artisanship of the Willards and their work with the Massachusetts shelf clock. Like the English bracket clock made by only a few Americans like Thomas Harland of Connecticut, William Lee of South Carolina, Joseph Pearsall of New York, and Thomas Parker of Philadelphia, the Massachusetts shelf clock was an expensive made-to-order or "bespoke" clock; and was already old fashioned in fashionable circles before the century was over. The first substantial break in quantitative production—affordable clocks—came when Eli Terry, a country artisan well trained in the making of cheap wood movements as well as those of expensive brass, designed a wooden wagon-on-the-wall which netted him a contract in 1807 for 4000 of them. It took him three years to complete the order, but his experience in mass producing wooden movements inspired the first popular shelf clock in America and the first manufacturing model for other industrializing firms. Chauncey Jerome, a Terry apprentice, competitor, admirer, and amateur historian, recorded Terry's accomplishments in his **History of the American Clock Business**, published in 1860:

> Mr. Eli Terry (in the year 1814), invented a Beautiful shelf clock made of wood which completely revolutionized the whole business. . . . This patent article Mr. Terry introduced, was called the Pillar Scroll Top Case. . . . This style of clock was liked very much and was made in large quantities, and for several years. . . . They were sold for fifteen dollars apiece. . . .

When Terry died, one obituary described him as "one of the most extensive clock manufacturers in the United States—a man of great mechanical genius, and the inventor of the mantle clock, so called, in contradistinction of the old fashioned case clock."

Many talented men followed Terry. Some began as his apprentices, and some began as his partners. Seven great clock companies developed by 1850 to produce the new shapes and new materials, the new movements, novelties, and revivals. Tall cases were then sometimes referred to as "Colonials"; pillar and scrolls were often called "Plymouths," after the Connecticut town in which the clock was most frequently manufactured. Business stimulated demand for clock makers and clock peddlars, and their numbers grew geometrically throughout the century. The nineteenth-century shelf-clock maker, in trying to reach the masses, had isolated and identified some of the requirements of men and machines. He had accumulated and utilized knowledge to make a product which satisfied others. In his effort to be successful, he added immeasurably to the history of novelty, imagination, and invention.

1. Grandfather (Tall Case) Clocks, pp. 49-57

3. Lantern Clocks, pp. 61-63

4. Wag-On-The-Walls, pp. 63-65

5. Regulators, pp. 65-70

6. Massachusetts Wall Clocks, pp. 70-73

7. Banjo (Patent) Timepieces, pp. 74-78

8. Gallery Clocks, pp. 78-82

9. Girandole and Diamond Head Timepieces,
pp. 82-85

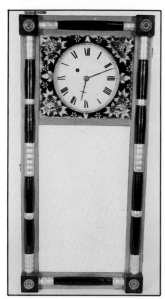

12. Schoolhouse Clocks, pp. 93-97

13. Calendar Clocks (wall),
pp. 97-100

14. Figure Eights, pp. 101-104

17. Advertising Clocks, pp. 110-12

18. Bracket Clocks, pp. 112-15

19. Massachusetts Shelf Clocks, pp. 115-19

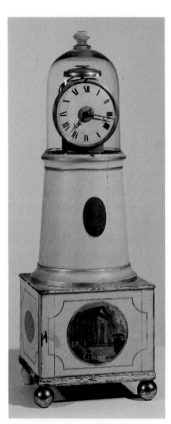

23. Lighthouse Timepieces,
pp. 133-36

24. Column Clocks, pp. 136-42

25. Double and Triple Deckers, pp. 143-47

26. Column and Stenciled Splat Clocks, pp. 147-51

30. Steeple (Sharp Gothic) Clocks, pp. 165-71

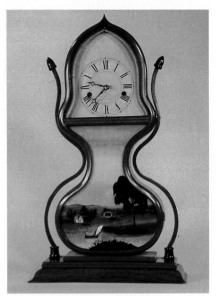

31. Acorn Clocks, pp. 171-74

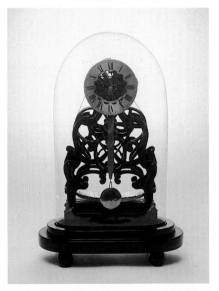

32. Skeleton Timepieces, pp. 174-75

35. Calendar Clocks (shelf), pp. 183-87

36. Blinking Eye Timepieces, pp. 187-90

37. Round Tops,
pp. 191-95

38. Pedimented Tops, pp. 195-98

43. Mantel Clock Variations, pp. 211-16

44. Cabinet (Gingerbread) Clocks, pp. 216-22

45. Blacks, pp. 222-28

46. Alarms, pp. 228-34

47. Art Nouveau Clocks, pp. 234-37

48. Mission Oak Clocks,
    pp. 237-39

1 Grandfather (Tall Case) Clocks

The first American tall-case designs, copied from the bold English Baroque style popular with seventeenth-century European tastemakers, were comprised of the "head"—an eighteenth-century term for a bonnet or hood—which housed the movement; the "pendulum case" or merely "case"—today called a "trunk," "body," "throat," or "waist"—which covered the wood or metal pendulum rod and bob; and the "base"—also called a pedestal or plinth—enclosing the space in which weights could drop to drive the movement. Even without feet the grandfather clock was usually never less than sixty-inches high. Whether the clocks came from Philadelphia, Boston, or Newport, the first case styles reflected a myriad of traditional, rather than innovative, furniture designs and ornament—flat or sarcophagus tops, case door bull's-eye glass, walnut veneer, lacquer, japanning, or inlay work, and a square or arched brass dial with dolphin, urn, or cherub spandrels decorating the four dial corners.

By the end of the Colonial period, flat and sarcophagus tops had been replaced by the broken arch and husky Rococo scrolls ending in carved rosettes. Engaged, fluted quarter columns and ogee bracket feet ornamented the case. The "newest fashion" introduced in the Federal period was characterized by straight tapered feet, inlay decoration, and a smaller scale in the proportioning of the head.

Clockmakers frequently ordered their cases from local cabinetmakers and sometimes sold their movements to them as well. Either clockmaker or cabinetmaker, then, was able to sell a grandfather clock with his own label and yet have made only movement or case.

Tall-clock movements were sometimes precision timekeepers. More often, however, they recorded one or a series of events like time, tide, day, date, month, and moon's age. The movements, usually of brass but possibly of iron or wood, were made of parts either imported or of domestic manufacture. When they ran for thirty hours, the winding was done by manually pulling up the weight and chain. When they ran for a week, a key in the winding square of the dial hole raised the weight.

Although the tall-case clockmaker was rarely the creator of all his own parts—not necessarily the maker of his own cases, the engraver or painter of his dials, the founder of the bell, or the merchant selling to the retail trade—his tall-case assemblage represents the first accurate timekeeper in the history of horological instruments and the most elegant piece of furniture in the colonial home.

1-O Grandfather Clock (color plate)
Benjamin Morris
New Britain, PA, 1787
H. 95", W. 18", D. 10"

Federal period, Chippendale influence, walnut case, fluted quarter columns, inlaid holly crown, date, flowers, stars, and initials "A.I.", carved flame and urn finials, keystone under center finial, raised fan on door, raised scrolled panel; double tiered, fluted quarter columns on base, bracket feet; landscape scene painted in dial arch; 8-day brass weight-driven movement; brass dial, day calendar, Roman chapters, time and strike. On dial "Benj. Morris/New Britain." **(A)**

Private Collection

1-1 Grandfather Clock
John Brand
Boston, MA, c. 1711
H. 73", W. 10½", D. 6½"

Colonial period, Baroque and Queen Anne influences, walnut and veneer flat-top case, bulls-eye glass in door, wood pendulum rod; 8-day brass and steel movement; brass dial with silver nameplate, and chased design, 2 cherubs and crown on each spandrel corner, separate second hand and dial, day calendar, raised iron Roman chapters, time and strike. This is the earliest tall case and clock made in America. On dial "J. Brand Boston." **(A)**

Private Collection

1-2 Grandfather Clock
John Wood, the Elder
Philadelphia, PA, c. 1730
H. 89", W. 18", D. 10¼"

Colonial period, Queen Anne influence, walnut case, inlay around sarcophagus top, cherub spandrels, inlay on door "T.T." and "M.L."; 30-hour weight-driven brass movement; brass dial, day calendar, Roman chapters, single hand, time and strike. On dial "John Wood/Philadelphia." On back panel in chalk "Cleaned Dec. 16, 1816. John Pittman." **(A)**

Private Collection

1-3 Grandfather Clock
Moses Wing
Windsor, CT, c. 1780
H. 80"

Federal period, Chippendale influence, cherry case, quarter round reeded columns on case, free-standing columns on head, bracket feet, carved fretwork, brass ball finials; silver chased dial, day calendar, separate second hand and dial, diamond-shaped hands, Roman chapters, time and strike. On dial "Moses Wing/ Windsor." **(C)**

H. and R. Sandor, Inc.

1-4 Grandfather Clock
Solomon Parke & Company
Philadelphia, PA, c. 1782
H. 95", W. 24"

Federal period, Chippendale influence, walnut case, quarter columns on case, free-standing columns on head, ogee bracket feet,
two brass urn finials, one wood-
shaped center finial; moon's age,
day calendar, separate second
hand and dial, Roman chapters,
time and strike. On dial "Solomon
Parke & Co./Philadª" (C)

Philip H. Bradley, Co.

1-5 Grandfather Clock
"Roxbury type"
Caleb Wheaton
Providence, RI, c. 1790
H. 91", W. 18½", D. 9½"

Federal period, Chippendale
and Hepplewhite influences, mahogany case with carved fretwork
on head, brass fluting on head
columns, wood inlay in head and
case doors and as fans on base
panel, quarter round fluted columns on case, bracket feet, brass
urns and eagle finials; white,
painted dial with house and landscape painted on dial arch, fans
matching the inlay fans in base
painted in corner spandrels, separate second hand and dial, diamond shaped hands, Arabic

chapters, time and strike. On dial
"Caleb Wheaton/ Providence."
(A)

Israel Sack, Inc., N.Y.C.

1-6 Grandfather Clock
Samuel Mulliken
Salem, MA, c. 1790
H. 79¾", W. 13¾", D. 8½"

Federal period, Chippendale influence, mahogany case, solid
shaped top, brass stop-fluted head columns, ogee feet; 8-day weight-
driven movement; white painted metal dial, separate second hand
and dial, day calendar, Roman chapters, time and strike. **(C)**

1-7 Grandfather Clock
"Marriage Clock"
George Hoff
Lancaster, PA, 1790
H. 7½", W. 17", D. 9½"

Federal period, Queen Anne influence, flat-top walnut case, quarter
columns, molding around base, sulphur inlay initials on case, sulphur
inlay parrot and date on door; thirty hour movement; pewter dial and
spandrels, Roman chapters, time and strike. On case "I.O" and "S.C."
On door, "1790." **(B)**

1-8 Grandfather Clock
"Roxbury type"
Simon Willard
Roxbury, MA, 1796-1805
H. 90"

Federal period, Chippendale and Hepplewhite influences, open fretwork on head, brass ball finials on fluted plinths, quarter round columns on case, fan quadrants on corners of door and base, ogee
bracket feet; white painted dial, moon's age in dial arch, calendar,
separate second hand and dial, time and strike. On dial "S. Willard."
On label "Clock Manufactory./ Simon Willard,/At his Clock Dial, in Rox-
bury/ Printed by J. Thomas, Jun. Worcester." Clock made for William
Lord, ship captain, of Kennebunkport. ME. With clock was a bill from
Simon Willard and Son, February 1, 1858, for repairs and cleaning. **(A)**

1-9 Grandfather Clock
John Nicholl
Belvedere, NJ, c. 1800
H. 92", W. 18", D. 10"

Federal period, Hepplewhite influence, mahogany and maple case with quarter round fluted columns, free-standing columns on head, arched dial, swan's neck scrolls with inlaid pinwheels on head, French tapered feet; white painted dial has flowers in spandrel corners, separate second hand and dial, moon's age in arch, Roman chapters, time and strike. On dial "John Nicholl/Belvedere, N.J." **(C)**

Philip H. Bradley, Co.

1-10 Grandfather Clock
Asa Hopkins
Litchfield, CT, 1800-20
H. 83"

Federal period, Hepplewhite influence, mahogany stained case with stylized curves around head; 30-hour wood movement, house and landscape painted in arch over dial, flowers painted in four spandrel corners; white painted dial, Arabic chapters, time and strike. On dial "A. Hopkins, Litchfield." **(D)**

National Museum of History and Technology, Smithsonian Institution

1-11 Grandfather Clock
David K. Akien
South Yarmouth, MA, c. 1820
H. 90½"

Empire period, Chippendale influence, solid-wood case, molded top, spindle-turned columns on head, quarter rounds on pendulum, wood ball finials, four turnip and ring feet; 8-day, brass weight-driven movement; white painted dial with American shields in spandrel corners and one larger shield in arch, separate second hand and dial, calendar, Roman chapters, time and strike. On dial "David K. Akien." **(D)**

Robert W. Skinner, Inc.

1-12 Grandfather Timepiece
"Regulator"
W.E. Harper
Philadelphia, PA, c. 1840
H. 90"

Victorian period, Egyptian influence, mummy-like shape, mahogany case with shape repeated for glass door; brass bezel and dial, Arabic chapters. On dial "W.E. Harper/Philadel^a **(D)**

Philip H. Bradley, Co.

1-13 Grandfather Clock
Waltham Clock Company
Waltham, MA, c. 1900
H. 95"

Victorian period, Chippendale and Lannuier influences, architectural mahogany case, ionic columns on head and case, oval beveled glass insert in door, carved paw feet, pediment on head; nine tube chime brass movement, three weights; silvered chapter ring, moon's age in arch over dial, brass spandrels and brass dial, Arabic chapters, time and strike. On dial "Waltham Clock Co." **(D)**

Robert W. Skinner, Inc.

1-14 Grandfather Clock
L. & J. G. Stickley
Fayetteville, NY, c. 1910
H. 80", W. 20", D. 12"

Modern period, Art Nouveau influence, white quarter-sawn oak case with flat top; brass weights and pendulum; copper repoussé door handle and dial, Arabic chapters, time and strike. **(C)**

Jordan-Volpe Gallery, New York

1-15 Grandfather Clock
Purcell & Elmslie
American, 1912
H. 88", W. 24¾"

Modern period, Art Nouveau influence, mahogany case with modernistic finials, lined designs and the suggestion of bracket feet; nine chrome-plated chimes; Arabic chapters, time, strike, and alarm. [Movement probably not American.] Designed for the Henry B. Babson House, Riverside, IL. **(B)**

The Art Institute of Chicago

2 | Grandmother (Dwarf Tall) Clocks

The "grandmother" clock, a modern name of American origin (it is also called "miniature tall case," "half-high," or "dwarf-tall") measures approximately three- to five-feet high, or two-thirds the size of a standard tall-case clock. Since its dial is in good view of a person lying in bed and the cord of its repeating mechanism within reach of the sleeper, the grandmother clock is supposed to have been designed for the bedroom, at least according to R. W. Symonds, authority on Thomas Tompion, the English "father of clockmakers."

Although grandmother clocks appeared in England in the seventeenth century, they were not made in America until the end of the eighteenth, and then only by a handful of tall-case makers like Benjamin Youngs of New York; Samuel Mulliken II, Reuben Tower, and Joshua Wilder of Massachusetts; and Nathaniel Hamlin of Maine. Grandmother clocks made in cities reflected the popular fretted and scrolled-top Federal fashion of the late eighteenth and early nineteenth centuries. In rural areas, however, the seventeenth-century flat top remained popular.

2-O Grandmother Timepiece (color plate)
John Bailey, Jr.
Hanover, NH, c. 1800
H. 44", W. 10½", D. 5½"

Federal period, Hepplewhite influence, walnut case, raised domed crest supporting small reeded pedestal with brass spread wing eagle; 8-day weight-driven movement; white painted iron dial with gilt scrolls in spandrel corners, Roman chapters, time only. On dial "John Bailey Jr./Hanover." **(A)**

Private Collection

2-1 Grandmother Timepiece
Joshua Wilder
Hingham, MA, 1810
H. 50¾", W. 10⅞, D. 5½"

Federal period, Hepplewhite influence, pine case painted red, dome top with brass ball finial, bracket feet; white painted dial and oval patera painted in spandrel corners, Arabic chapters, time only. On dial "Joshua Wilder/Hingham." **(A)**

H. & R. Sandor, Inc.

**2-2 Grandmother Timepiece
Attributed to Samuel Mulliken
Concord, MA, c. 1810
H. 48", 10¼"**

Federal period, Chippendale influence, pine case with small shaped door, flat top, bracket feet; brass dial, pewter hands, Roman chapters, time only. **(C)**

Sotheby Parke Bernet, Inc.

**2-3 Grandmother Clock
Reuben Tower
Hingham, MA, 1816
H. 47½", W. 11", D. 6"**

Empire period, Hepplewhite influence, painted grained case simulating mahogany, raised wooden crest with brass ball and eagle finial, American flag on door probably painted in the late 19th century; white painted dial with American shield painted in spandrel corners, swag painted in arch over dial, Roman chapters, time and strike. On dial "Reuben Tower Hingham." **(A)**

Israel Sack, Inc., N.Y.C.

dial, Roman chapters, time only. **(D)**

Sotheby Parke Bernet, Inc.

2-4 Grandmother Timepiece
Maker Unknown
New England, 1810-20
H. 53¼ ", W. 11¾ "

Empire period, Hepplewhite influence, pyramid-shaped mahogany case, French tapered feet, glass pendulum bob oval in base, brass ball finial on plinth above dial, brass bezel; white painted

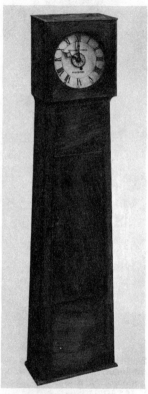

2-5 Grandmother Timepiece
Benjamin Youngs
Watervliet, NY, c. 1820
H. 50 ", W. 10 "

Empire period, Shaker influence, polished walnut case, Roman chapters, separate alarm dial, diamond-shaped hand, time and alarm. On dial "Benjamin Youngs Watervliet." **(C)**

Index of American Design, National Gallery of Art

**2-6 Grandmother Clock
"Roxbury type"
Joshua Wilder
Hingham, MA, c. 1821
H. 50¾", W. 10⅞", D. 5½"**

Empire period, Hepplewhite influence, mahogany case with typical Massachusetts curved head and open carved fretwork, tapered feet, quarter columns, bold brass ball finials on plinths; white painted dial, fruit and basket painted in dial arch and scallop shells in spandrel corners, diamond-shaped hands, Arabic chapters, time and strike. On dial "Warranted by/Joshua Wilder/ Hingham." On inside label "Manufactured for Martin Fearing by Joshua Wilder 1821." **(A)**

Israel Sack, Inc., N.Y.C.

II WALL CLOCKS

3 | Lantern Clocks

The lantern clock—usually a thirty-hour weight-driven timekeeper with a single hand—was called by the old English Clockmakers' Company a "brass" or "house" clock, and in inventories it was referred to as a "lantern," "chamber," "birdcage," "Cromwellian," or "bedpost" clock.

Although there are no lantern clocks known to have been made in

America except for the stamped sheet-brass torchlight lantern clock first used in the 1800s in midnight parades and picnics, seventeenth-century inventories list them as having been brought over by the first colonists. These early clocks were small, rectangular, and metallic, and were based on the Gothic iron-turret clock which hung from an iron loop attached to the wall by a spike. The pendulum, fitted to the clock after 1657, swung between spurs at the back. Lantern clocks could easily be carried, unwarped, overseas. Unlike the wooden works and wooden cases of other early timekeepers, they did not swell, splinter, or rot. The lantern clock thus spanned the gap between the sixteenth-century balance wheel and the seventeenth-century pendulum, between the English timekeepers and production of the first American ones, between exposed movements and hooded ones. The lantern clock was England's first national clock case style; as more and more Englishmen emigrated to the New World, it also became America's first timekeeper.

3-0 Lantern Clock (color plate)
John Aleward
England, c. 1690
H. 15 ", W. 5¼ ", D. 5¼ "

Pilgrim period, William and Mary influence, engraved brass case with five finials and exposed bell, dolphins and flowers span three frets across top; 30-hour brass movement with one weight; brass dial engraved with flowers, one hand only, Roman chapters, time and strike. On front fret "John Aleward, Fecit." **(C)**

Private Collection

3-1 Lantern Clock
Thomas Knifton
Lothbury, London, 1680-1725
H. 15½ ", W. 5¼ ", D. 5¼ "

Pilgrim and Colonial periods, William and Mary influence, brass works, case, and finial; fretwork above dial has dolphin and flower decorations, ball feet so that clock could stand on a bracket as well as hang from a hook; brass dial, hour hand only, time and strike. On dial "Thomas Knifton at the . . . Lothbury London." **(C)**

Old Sturbridge Village, Inc.

3-2 Lantern Clock
Bradley and Hubbard Manufac-
turing Company
Meriden, CT, c. 1885
H. 13", W. 6"

Victorian period, Gothic and
William and Mary influences,
stamped sheet-brass case with
colored convex glass, candle behind glass dial reflects time;
30-hour lever, balance wheel
movement; glass dial, arrow
hands, time and strike; used for
nighttime parades. **(E)**

B. C. & R. Roan, Inc.

4 | Wag-On-The-Walls

The wag-on-the-wall or "hang-up" clock—with a dial in brass,
painted sheet iron, or wood—began as little more than a thirty-hour
lantern clock with a square dial plate, which had been hung without
its four metal or wooden sides and with its pendulum and weights
hanging exposed below the movement. Even when a short wooden
hood or head was devised to protect the movement, the pendulum
and weights still remained uncovered.

A few American-made brass hang-ups appeared in the first half of
the eighteenth century with dials measuring six- to eight-inches
square. The dials increased in size, reaching ten to twelve inches, by
the end of the eighteenth century. By the nineteenth century Eli Terry
and Seth Thomas were making wooden dials covered in paper and
painted with floral or landscape patterns, and these were used as
wall-hanging or tall-case movements. The importation of inexpensive German Black Forest wags, sometimes coming over as cuckoo
variations, probably inspired the design of caseless, wooden works
in America. But it was Eli Terry's first contract for 4000 wag movements
(to be completed between 1807 and 1809 for Levi and Edward
Porter) which profoundly affected American horology and the
industrial world. By accepting this time-bound contract, Terry was
forced to find faster ways of working. With imagination and mechanical genius, he used water to power his machinery, and machinery

to cut down the tooling of wheel teeth, the heart of movement making. Thus the wag-on-the-wall led indirectly to the beginnings of the American clock industry.

4-0 Wag-on-the-Wall Timepiece (color plate)
Isaac Blasdel
Chester, NH, c. 1750
H. 8½ "

Colonial period, Queen Anne influence; crown gear escapement, exposed pendulum-driven movement; arched brass dial plate, cast-brass spandrels, single hand, Roman chapters, time only. **(C)**

Old Sturbridge Village, Inc.

4-1 Wag-on-the-Wall Timepiece
Eben Hanscom
Newport (RI or England), c. 1700
H. 6½ ", W. 4½ ", D. 4½ "

Colonial period, Queen Anne influence, brass case, works, cast spandrels, and ball feet; crown gear escapement; arched brass dial plate, hour hand only, Roman chapters, time and strikes once on the hour; weight-driven. On arch dial "Eben:/Hanscom./Newport./pagnell.'" **(D)**

Shelburne Museum, Inc.

4-2 Wag-on-the-Wall Clock
Eli Terry, Attribution
Probably East Windsor, CT,
c. 1790
H. 16 ", W. 11 "

Federal period, Colonial influence, wooden works, tin weights filled with pebbles, metal pendulum; white painted wood dial, ship and flower sprigs painted in arch of dial plate, flowers also painted in spandrel corners, Roman chapters, separate second hand and dial, separate date of the month hand and dial, time and strike. **(E)**

Index of American Design, National Gallery of Art, Washington

4-3 Wag-on-the-Wall Clock
Seth Thomas
Thomaston, CT, c. 1870
H. 36 ", W. 17 "

Victorian period, Chippendale in-fluence, hooded wall clock with arched dial plate and moon's age mechanism, with scrolled pediment ending in carved ro-settes, keystone above dial, single wood finial; free-standing columns, short board below head; weights and pendulum ex-posed; white painted dial with scrolls in spandrel corners, Arabic chapters, time and strike. On dial "Seth Thomas." **(F)**

B. C. & R. Roan, Inc.

4-4 Wag-on-the-Wall Clock
Seth Thomas
Thomaston, CT, c. 1870
H. 36 ", W. 17 ", Dial 6¾ "

Victorian period, Chippendale influence, walnut hood; moon's age mechanism; white, painted dial with flowers painted in four spandrel corners, Arabic chapters, time and strike. **(F)**

4-5 Wag-on-the-Wall Clock
"Study No. 3"
Waterbury Clock Company
Waterbury, CT, c. 1895
H. 22¼ ", dial 8 "

Victorian period, oak hood, glass sides; 8-day weight movement; silver dial, time and gong strike. Listed in Montgomery Ward & Company catalogue of 1895 for $8.75. **(F)**

5 | Regulators

Technically the term "regulator" has only one horological meaning. According to clock historian Willis Milham it is a high-grade precision instrument, nearly always a pendulum timepiece with a compensating factor of gridiron, mercury jars, or nickel-steel alloys attached to the pendulum to counteract temperature changes. A wooden rod pendulum treated to resist the climate, a large zinc bob, a dead-beat escapement, maintaining power attached to the driving mechanism, and weights or an electrical self-winding mechanism make up the other essential elements. The first regulator timepiece was probably made around 1670, although the term itself was not used until the middle of the eighteenth century.

Practically speaking, the term "regulator" has also been applied to the long-drop wall case in which the regulator movement has most often been found. Although regulator movements had been placed in tall-clock cases too, they functioned more reliably hanging on the wall where the vibrations from human activity were considerably less in evidence. Since the name "regulator" implies precision, quality, and subsequently a costly price tag, collectors are urged to differentiate between the regulator with a quality movement and the long, hanging regulator-type case with a common mechanism which provides the "look" of a quality timepiece without the performance of one.

The first American regulators were used in astronomical laboratories, churches, and public buildings. William Claggett's timepiece, (5-1) made for the Seventh Day Baptist Church in Newport, Rhode Island, in 1732, has a long-drop regulator-type case typical of an English model owned in 1714 by Sir Francis Forbes and typical of one made by Pratt of West Hampton, England, about 1760, and of one made by Thomas Moore of Ipswich and Suffolk, England. These handsome black and gilt muraled pieces are the first models commonly associated with this horological category.

Two later adapted case styles evoking different historical periods and different decorative tastes came to be associated with nineteenth-century regulators hanging in America's watch factories, jewelry stores, and railroad stations. One style, with carved Baroque pediments and lower adorned brackets, was called the "Vienna" regulator (5-5). It was inspired by the Gustav Becker examples made in Lower Saxony. The other style, with its unadorned classical and simple Queen Anne curve, came in E. Howard and Company banjos or in graceful figure eights.

5-O Regulator Timepiece (color plate)
"No. 1"
Seth Thomas Clock Company
Thomaston, CT, c. 1870
H. 53 ", W. 13 ", D. 4½ ", Dial and frame 20 "

Victorian period, Queen Anne influence, oak and veneer long drop case, black, gilt, and vertical pendulum bob oval painted on glass tablet; 8-day, brass weight-driven movement with Graham deadbeat escapement; white painted dial, separate second hand and dial, Roman chapters, time only. Listed in 1884 catalogue for $22.50. **(E)**

5-1 Regulator-type Timepiece
William Claggett
Newport, RI, c. 1732
H. 68", Dial 26"

Colonial period, Queen Anne influence, walnut and tulip poplar, octagonal frame and long drop case, oriental bird and tree painted on japanned, black and gilt case, oval pendulum bob glass and bottom finial on lower case; dead beat anchor escapement, wood pendulum rod; octagonal dial, Roman chapters, engraved fleur-de-lis between hours, painted outer seconds dial with Arabic numerals, time only. On dial "William Clagget/Newport." Made for Seventh Day Baptist Church. **(B)**

Newport Historical Society

5-2 Regulator Timepiece
Aaron Willard, Jr.
Boston, MA, c. 1823
H. 29"

Empire period, classical influence, mahogany, long drop case; brass works, weight driven; white, painted dial, Roman chapters, moon-shaped hands, time only. **(D)**

5-3 Regulator Variation Timepiece
"Floor Model"
E. Howard & Company
Boston, MA, c. 1845
H. 95¼"

Victorian period, Gothic influence, mahogany case, jeweled, precision 8-day weight-driven movement, single-vial mercury pendulum; silver dial, Arabic chapters, three separate hands and dials for hours, minutes and seconds, time only. On dial "Regulator/E. Howard & Co. Boston." **(C)**

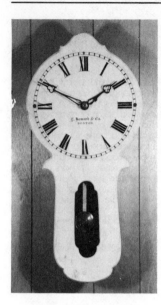

5-4 Regulator Timepiece
E. Howard & Company
Boston, MA, c. 1850
H. 30", Dial 14¾"

Victorian period, marble case; 8-day brass weight-powered movement; white marble dial, Roman chapters, time only. On dial and on movement "E. Howard & Co. Boston." Still illustrated in 1874 catalogue as "No. 28". **(D)**

W. G. Harding

5-5 Regulator Timepiece
"No. 59 Timepiece, Vienna Model"
E. Howard & Company
Roxbury or Boston, MA, c. 1870
H. 39", W. 10", D. 5"

Victorian period, Baroque and Chippendale influences, black walnut, ebony, and maple case, three turned wooden finials, and three carved drop finials; 8-day movement, invar rod pendulum, weight behind maple panel; white painted dial, Roman chapters, moon-shaped hands, time only. On dial "E. Howard & Co./Boston." **(C)**

Private Collection

5-6 Regulator Timepiece
James William Worn
Philadelphia, PA, c. 1890
H. 49", W. 19¼", D. 10"

Victorian period, round top oak case; Graham dead-beat escapement with jeweled pallets, mercury compensated pendulum, off-center brass shell weight; silvered brass dial, Roman chapters, separate second hand and dial, time only. On dial "James William Worn/Philadelphia." Regulator once hung in main waiting room of Pennsylvania Railroad Station in Philadelphia. **(B)**

NAWCCM, Inc.

5-7 Regulator Timepiece
"Carlton"
Waterbury Clock Company
Waterbury, CT, c. 1895
H. 32", Dial 12"

Victorian period, classical influence, solid oak veneer case, octagon dial frame, long drop; 8-day movement, wood pendulum rod; white painted dial, Roman chapters for time, Arabic numerals for larger outer calendar ring, separate calendar hand, time only. Listed in 1895 Sears, Roebuck & Company catalogue for $5.85 **(E)**

5-8 Regulator Timepiece
Seth Thomas Clock Company
Thomaston, CT, c. 1900
H. 44", W. 14", D. 5"

Victorian period, press-molded oak case with brass cornice, wood-turned finials, free-standing columns with brass bases and Corinthian capitals; trapezoidal brass movement, Graham dead beat escapement, Harrison maintaining power mechanism and a pin crutch, 8-day movement; metal dial, spade hands, Roman chapters, separate second hand and dial, time only. On front plate is stamped "407"; on back plate is stamped "Seth-Thomas New York." **(E)**

NAWCCM, Inc.

**5-9 Regulator Timepiece
"No. 2"
Seth Thomas Clock Company
Thomaston, CT, c. 1900
H. 36 ", W. 9¾ ", D. 5 ", Dial 15½ "**

Victorian period, round top oak case; rectangular movement, Graham dead-beat escapement, a Harrison maintaining power mechanism, pin crutch, pendulum hanging from movement mounting block on case back; white painted dial, Roman chapters, spade hands, separate second hand and dial, time only. On dial ''P.R.R. 0090/Seth Thomas.'' **(E)**

NAWCCM, Inc.

**5-10 Regulator Timepiece
"Columbia"
New Haven Clock Company
New Haven, CT, c. 1911
H. 49½ ", W. 13 ", D. 6½ "**

Modern period, Vienna-type oak case with press carving and gilt ornament of a classical head applied to cornice; 30-day movement with two mainsprings, and therefore two wind squares on dial to power movement, anchor recoil escapement, escape wheel outside back plate; white painted dial, Roman chapters, separate seconds hand and dial, time only. On dial ''Thirty Day.'' Stamped on movement ''New Haven trademark, patent dates Feb. 23, 1890, Dec. 6, 1883 (England), and Jan. 19, 1892.'' **(E)**

NAWCCM, Inc.

6 | Massachusetts Wall Timepieces

The Massachusetts wall timepiece, also called a "thirty-hour" or a "Grafton wall clock," was the first in a series of small, two-foot high, moderately priced, uniquely American timekeepers to come on the market in the eighteenth century. Though emulating the very expensive American bracket clock copied from English models, and with its scrolled feet seeming to stand on a separate shelf, the Massachusetts wall timepiece is in fact a case and bracket all in one piece. A dead-beat escapement and short pendulum on the verge shaft are part of its power-control complex. It runs for a day and is generally found without a second hand, day of the month indicator, or striking train, all features which made it less complicated and less costly than other timekeepers of its day. This automatic "once-on-the-hour striker"—a step between the **timepiece**, which never strikes, and the **clock**, which strikes the full number of hours—is classified here as a timepiece, since it is without the extra train commonly associated with clocks. The case is a product of the transition from the Colonial to the Federal style and originated in the shops of Simon or Aaron Willard and possibly in the shop of the Mullikin family.

6-O Massachusetts Wall Timepiece (color plate)
Simon Willard
Grafton, MA, c. 1780
H. 24 ", W. 8 ", D. 3¾ "

Federal period, Chippendale and Hepplewhite influences, mahogany case and bracket in one piece (though scroll feet give it the appearance of a shelf Bracket clock), carved wooden fretwork across top, brass urn-shaped finials; 30-hour movement, heavy lead weight recessed at back for pendulum swing, exposed bell; brass dial probably imported, day calendar, separate second hand and dial, Roman chapters, time only. **(A)**

Peter W. Eliot

6-1 Massachusetts Wall Timepiece
Simon Willard
Grafton, MA, c. 1770
H. 22 ", W. 7 "

Colonial period, Chippendale influence, mahogany case with open carved fretwork, kidney-shaped glass door, two brass urn-shaped finials; 30-hour weight movement; cast-brass dial, Roman chapters, time only. Strikes once an hour. **(A)**

6-2 Massachusetts Wall Timepiece
Timothy Sibley
Sutton, MA, c. 1780
H. 22 ", W. 7⅞ ", D. 3¾ "

Federal period, Chippendale and Hepplewhite influences, wood case, flat top, suggestion of a bracket at the bottom, kidney-shaped glass; engraved brass dial plate cut in same kidney shape as glass, triangular brass cutouts in spandrel corners, Roman chapters, time only. On dial "Tim⁰ Sibley, Sutton." Although Col. Timothy Sibley is listed in Palmer's Book of American Clocks as the father of the clockmaker Asa, it is assumed the father was also a clockmaker. His name appears above dial. It is possible, however, that the name refers to the owner. **(A)**

Israel Sack, Inc., N.Y.C.

6-3 Massachusetts Wall Timepiece
Simon Willard
Roxbury, MA, c. 1780
H. 43½ ", W. 10¼ ", D. 4¾ "

Federal period, Chippendale influence, mahogany case and fret-work, two brass urn finials; solid-brass gears, 30-hour movement, version of deadbeat escapement; brass dial, Roman chapters, separate second hand and dial, date of month, time only. Strikes once an hour. On dial "Simon Willard." **(A)**

6-4 Massachusetts Wall Timepiece
Aaron Willard
Grafton, MA, c. 1780
H. 28", W. 8¾", D. 3½"

Federal period, Chippendale influence, mahogany case and open fretwork; 30-hour movement with a version of deadbeat escapement, pendulum hanging directly from verge shaft; metal dial, Roman chapters, time only. Clock strikes once on the hour. On dial "A. Willard Grafton." **(A)**

6-5 Massachusetts Wall Timepiece
"Patent Timepiece"
Simon Willard
Grafton, MA, c. 1785
H. 24½", W. 8⅜", D. 3¾"

Federal period, Chippendale and Hepplewhite influences, mahogany case, carved rope edges on upper section, wood urn-shaped finials, modified kidney-shaped glass, exposed brass bell and striking hammer; top hole meant for second hand, one lead weight, recessed at back, pendulum hangs from verge shaft; brass dial, Roman chapters, time only. On dial "Ab loc . . . Momento Pendit Eternitas/Simon Willard." **(A)**

Sotheby Parke Bernet

7 | Banjo (Patent) Timepieces

The banjo timepiece, called by its designer Simon Willard the "patent timepiece," was invented about 1795 and patented in 1802. Except for the substitution of the common anchor-recoil escapement for the more precise dead-beat escapement, the banjo reflects the small movement and small case of Willard's Massachusetts wall timepiece. The banjo was innovative in the sense that it could be mass produced, and although there is some question about the accuracy of John Ware Willard's statement that Simon Willard himself made 4000 movements, the number of banjos extant attests to their having been made in great numbers. The banjo fitted the pocketbook of the rising middle class and offered a gilded, carved elegance in its new combination of classical acanthus and anthemion leaves, volutes and scrolls, and eagles seated or with spread wings.

Banjos were often used commemoratively. Famous battles were painted on the base glass panels by Aaron Willard and others. Gilding often signaled that the timepiece was being presented at a special event like a wedding or high public appointment. Like the furniture and architecture of the period, the banjo was decorative but light, taking up much less visible and actual space than did the tall-case clock. The base was typically rectangular, the circular top a variation of the French lyre and the French and English balloon clocks. Having painted scenes on the pendulum case and base tablets led to its also being classified by some as a "mural" timepiece. The finial at the top was in the shape of an acorn, ball, or eagle in brass or wood. The craftsman's choice of surface decoration, however, is secondary to the beauty of the Banjo form itself.

One manufacturer, Edward Howard, made at least six banjo variations. Manufacturing first with his partner David Porter Davis, Howard made a unique banjo case and also cases which looked like the original Willard type. The earliest Howard & Davis banjos, made in 1842, had rectilinear bases and were unnumbered. The side-curve banjos, made by E. Howard & Company starting in 1857, were available in sizes that were numbered one through five, the former being the largest and measuring fifty-inches high with a twelve-inch dial and an eight-inch pendulum; the latter being the smallest and measuring twenty-nine inches high with a seven-inch dial and a three-inch pendulum. The glass tablets were decorated in black and gold leaf; the bezels were wood.

When Davis left the firm, banjos continued to be produced in the same patterns. The addition of red pigment to the glass tablet at the base seems to have been the only visible design change.

7-0 Banjo Timepiece (color plate)
Simon Willard
Roxbury, MA, c. 1802-15
H. 43", W. 10", D. 3½"

Federal period, Hepplewhite and French influences, mahogany and glass case; typical Simon Willard white, blue, and gilt geometric designs surrounding flowers and vines painted on glass case panel, bell flowers on glass base; brass side brackets join dial to base; brass bezel, spread gilt eagle above dial; T-bridge escapement; white painted dial, Roman chapters, time only. On base glass "S. Willard's/ Patent." Thomas Jefferson signed the patent and encouraged Willard to file for it. **(A)**

Israel Sack, Inc., N.Y.C.

7-1 Banjo Clock
Benjamin Willard, Jr.
Lexington, MA, c. 1800
H. 25", W. 11½"

Federal period, mahogany, neoclassical female painted on pedestal glass; 8-day movement, pull cord for strike repeating located at four o'clock on side of case; white painted dial, Roman chapters, time and strike. On dial "Benjamin Willard, Jr./Lexington." **(B)**

7-2 Banjo Timepiece
Lemuel Curtis
Concord, MA, c. 1810
H. 39"

Federal period, classical influence, gilt wood case, scrolled design painted on middle glass tablet, allegorical Aurora painted on lower glass tablet, brass side brackets, gilt wood pedestal, gilded wood finial; white painted dial, Roman chapters, time only. **(B)**

7-3 Banjo Timepiece
"Presentation Model"
Aaron Willard
Boston, MA, c. 1812-23
H. 38", W. 10⅛"

Empire period, classical influence, gilded wood case, brass side brackets, gilded wood finial, and gilded bracket-like form below base with gilded balls, 1812 naval battle scene painted on base glass, shield, eagle, and designs painted on center glass tablet, brass bezel; 8-day movement; white painted dial, Roman chapters, time only. **(A)**

7-4 Banjo Timepiece
Aaron Willard
Boston, MA, c. 1824
H. 30"

Empire period, classical influence, mahogany case, glass case and base panel painted and gilded; Mt. Vernon pictured on base; gilded cone finial above dial; white painted dial, Roman chapters, time only. On dial "Willard, Boston." **(B)**

The National Museum of History and Technology, Smithsonian Institution

7-5 Banjo Timepiece
J. Dyer (or Dyar)
MA or VT, c. 1825
H. 43½", W. 11"

Empire period, classical influence, cherry case with rope-turned gilt engaged columns, gilt wood bezel, eagle on urn-shaped finial, small glass panel in door, gilt balls and bracket effect below; 8-day weight-driven movement; white painted iron dial, Roman chapters, time only. On dial "Warranted by J. Dyar." **(D)**

Robert W. Skinner, Inc.

7-6 Banjo Timepiece
John J. Low & Company
Boston, MA, c. 1828
H. 39½"

Empire period, classical influence, painted stenciled case, glass case panel painted with landscape scene, base panel also painted, eagle on ball above dial, brass side pieces; white painted dial, Roman chapters, time only. On dial "John J. Low & Co./Boston." **(A)**

Israel Sack, Inc., N.Y.C.

7-7 Banjo Timepiece
G.D. Hatch, manufacturer
Horace Tifft, movement maker
North Attleboro, MA, c. 1830

Empire period, classical influence, mahogany and veneer case, unusually designed mahogany side brackets and finial, black and gold painted tablets, gilt-edged pendulum bob oval; 8-day brass weight-driven movement; white painted dial, Roman chapters, time only. On dial "G. D. Hatch." On weight "H. T." [Horace Tifft). **(B)**

Robert W. Skinner, Inc.

7-8 Banjo Timepiece
"Modified Banjo"
Simon Willard
Roxbury, MA, 1832
H. 72", W. 18"

Empire period, classical influence, splayed, mahogany veneer case, clear glass door; brass movement, mercury compensated, seconds pendulum; white painted dial, separate second hand and dial, Roman chapters, time only. Inscribed, "Made by Simon Willard in his 79th year." **(B)**

American Clock and Watch Museum

7-9 Banjo Timepiece
Chauncey Jerome
New Haven, CT, c. 1850
H. 51"

Victorian period, classical influence, dark walnut case with clear glass on pendulum case, painted black and gilt in base glass; white painted dial, Roman chapters, second hand, time only. On dial "C. Jerome." **(D)**

The National Museum of History and Technology, Smithsonian Institution

7-10 Banjo Timepiece
E. Howard & Company
Boston, MA, c. 1860
H. 29", Dial 7"

Victorian period, Federal and Empire influences, mahogany-stained imitation rosewood case, glass and base panels painted in geometric forms using black, red, and gilt; recoil escapement, No. 5; white dial, Roman chapters, time only. On dial "E. Howard & Co. Boston." **(D)**

Samuel M. Freeman 2nd

8 | Gallery Timepieces

The round, (or round-cornered octagonal) hanging eight-day spring-driven timepiece commonly called a gallery clock, made in England by John Arnold about 1790, did not appear in the American horological craft until the Willards of Massachusetts began to make them almost two decades later. Although Simon Willard's gallery timepieces for the Roxbury and Dorchester churches were decorated with spread-wing eagles, gilt beads, and simulated lower brackets, most of the galleries which followed appeared in simple, functional, unadorned models. Brewster, Ingraham, and Jerome (of Connecticut) and Howard and Davis (of Massachusetts) produced unpainted walnut or chestnut frames as well as corrugated or ruffled gilded frames. Later in the nineteenth century the E. Howard Watch and Clock Company offered twenty-four-inch marble gallery timepieces and long-drop models (5-4). Chauncey Jerome advertised his gallery models as "detached lever" or "gallery day" timepieces. They were popular items and were listed in catalogues and circulars distributed in England and America during the 1850s.

8-O Gallery Timepieces (color plate)
Elias Ingraham and Company
Bristol, CT, c. 1875-88

Clockwise from top:

Dial 23″, with frame 33″
Victorian period, classical influence, round gilt frame; 8-day movement with elongated plate; white painted dial, Roman chapters, time only. On label "E. Ingraham & Co./Bristol, Ct." **(F)**

Dial 13″, with frame 21″
Victorian period, classical influence, round chestnut frame; 8-day movement with enlongated plate; white painted dial, Roman chapters, time only. On label "E. Ingraham and Company/Bristol, Connecticut." **(F)**

Dial 11″, with frame 19″
Victorian period, classical influence, chestnut frame; 8-day movement with elongated plate; white painted dial, Roman chapters, time only. On label "E. Ingraham & Co./Bristol, Ct." **(F)**

Dial 13″, with frame 21″
Victorian period, classical influence, round walnut frame with stain resembling cherry wood; 8-day movement with elongated plate; white painted dial, Roman chapters, time only. On label "E. Ingraham & Co./Bristol, Ct." **(F)**

American Clock and Watch Museum

8-1 Gallery Timepiece
Simon Willard
Roxbury, MA, c. 1804
H. 78″, Dial 36″

Federal period, classical influence, wooden frame carved by John Doggett and painted in gold leaf, spread wing eagle on ball on plinth, gilt ball strings, bracket is part of gallery; white painted wooden dial, Roman chapters, time only. Made for First Church of Roxbury. **(A)**

Willard House and Clock Museum

8-2 Gallery Timepiece
"East-West Model"
Elisha Brewster and Elias and
Andrew Ingraham
Bristol, CT, c. 1850
D. 16"

Victorian period, classical influence, round wood frame; 8-day brass mainspring movement, pendulum suspended from pillar on case back board; dial removed to display horizontal movement, time only. On label "Patent Spring Eight Day/Gallery and Office Clocks/ Manufactured by Brewster & Ingrahams, Bristol, Conn. . . . Elihu Geer, Hartford." **(E)**

NAWCCM, Inc.

8-3 Gallery Timepiece
E. Ingraham & Company
Bristol, CT, c. 1869
D. of dial 10"

Victorian period, round molded walnut frame; 8-day spring movement; white painted dial, Roman chapters, time only. Listed in 1860-80 catalogues for $7.00. **(F)**

8-4 Gallery Timepiece
Waterbury Clock Company
Waterbury, CT, c. 1875
D. of dial 9"

Victorian period, classical influence, molded octagonal walnut case, brass bezel; brass spring movement; paper dial, Roman chapters, slow-fast mechanism, separate second hand and dial, time only. On dial "Manufactured by Waterbury Clock Co., U.S.A." **(F)**

NAWCCM, Inc.

8-5 Gallery Clock
Seth Thomas Clock Company
Thomaston, CT, c. 1875
D. of dial 13"

Victorian period, classical influence, simulated painted burl walnut decahedral case, brass bezel; brass spring movement; white painted dial, Roman chapters, separate second hand and dial, slow-fast mechanism, time and strike. On dial "Seth Thomas." **(F)**

NAWCCM, Inc.

8-6 Gallery Clock
E. N. Welch Manufacturing
Company
Bristol, CT, c. 1880
D. 11"

Victorian period, classical influence, rosewood veneer, octagonal dial frame; lever escapement, slow-fast regulator; white painted dial, Roman chapters, separate second hand and dial, time and strike. On dial "Patent Lever Escapement." **(E)**

B. C. & R. Roan, Inc.

8-7 Gallery Clock
New Haven Clock Company
New Haven, CT, c. 1880
D. 20"

Victorian period, molded gilded dial frame; 8-day spring movement; white painted dial, Roman chapters, time and strike. **(F)**

**8-8 Gallery Timepiece
"Electric Time"
Maker Unknown
Place Unknown
19th century
Dial 12 ", with frame 19 "**

Victorian period, wooden frame with scallop design, movement mounted on 3 " brass plate with a 3-arm holding piece which secures electromagnet designed to advance the minute hand when given an impulse; white painted dial, Roman chapters, time only. On dial "Electric Time."

The National Museum of History and Technology, Smithsonian Institution

9 | Diamond Head and Girandole Timepieces

Two variations of the banjo timepiece—the diamond head and the girandole—appeared between 1810 and 1816, the girandole probably invented by Lemuel Curtis, a disciple of the Willard family, and patented in 1816 even though some scholars still dispute Curtis's patent. Like most banjos, these variations are timepieces; that is, they have no strike trains; they have eight-day movements; and they have common anchor recoil escapements.

The diamond-head case is often a delightful contrast of dark mahogany wood and light painted-glass panels. The "girandole," a name chosen in the twentieth century from fashionable French convex and gilt looking glasses, is actually an original Boston design, as is the diamond head. (Curtis did not move to Vermont until 1821.) Of all the timepieces, clocks, and watches which Curtis and his partner Joseph Dunning sold in Burlington, Vermont, they chose the girandole to illustrate their work in newspaper advertisements. With the revival of interest in the cultural and intellectual past characteristic of the Federal and Empire periods, Curtis properly chose classical and allegorical figures to paint on the girandole glass panels. Events that enflamed the popular imagination during the War of 1812—MacDonough's victory on Lake Champlain, Perry's victory, and the capture of the "Macedonian"—were also depicted, as were popular biblical stories. The designs were taken from engravings by artisans like John Ritto Penniman who supplied Curtis, the Willards, and others with scenic decorations. Lemuel's brother Samuel, who worked on mirrors and looking glasses, also painted and gilded Lemuel's dials and tablets. These "rich parlour timepieces," as they were described in newspaper ads, must have pleased no more than the handful of customers who could then afford elegant clocks and timepieces.

9-O Girandole Timepiece (color plate, left)
Lemuel Curtis
Concord, MA, c. 1820-25
H. 45", W. 12"

Empire period, classical influence, gilded wood case, allegorical figures of peace and justice with the American shield painted on upper glass, Biblical scene ("Elisha Restores the Shunamite's Son to Life") painted on lower convex glass, gilt eagle on ball above dial, brass brackets on sides; white painted dial, unique looped hands effecting a double serpentine design, Roman chapters, time only. **(A)**

Diamond Head Timepiece (color plate, right)
Jabez Baldwin
Salem or Boston, MA, 1810-19
H. 39", W. 11¾₆", D. 4⅛

Federal-Empire period, classical influence, dark mahogany, and veneer over white pine; case panel reeded at top and on plinth, topped by gilded cone-shaped finial, rectangular base, painted glass panel; white painted dial with gilt scrolls in spandrel corners and one American shield painted in top corner, Roman chapters, time only. Painted on lower glass "Jabez Baldwin." **(A)**

Henry Francis du Pont Winterthur Museum

9-1 Diamond Head Timepiece
Daniel Monroe
Concord, MA, c. 1810-30
H. 28¾", W. 11", D. 4"

Federal and Empire periods, mahogany case, inlaid chain design bordering base, case, dial door, and plinth above, pendulum case and base panels painted in white, light blue, and gilt, brass brackets on sides, brass feet unique to this clock, giving it the versatility of being able to be placed on a shelf, painted cone finial; white enameled dial, American shield painted in top, scrolls painted in corners, Roman chapters, time and strike. **(A)**

Israel Sack, Inc., N.Y.C.

9-2 Girandole Timepiece
Attributed to Lemuel Curtis
Concord, MA, 1816
H. 45 "

Empire period, classical influence, gilt wood, brass, and glass clock; glass in pendulum case and lower convex balloon shape painted, the latter with a view of the Mitchell & Freeman's China and Glass Warehouse on Chatham Street, Boston (the identical scene appears on a blue Staffordshire plate made by William Adams at Stoke, England), gilt spread eagle on ball and plinth, brass side brackets, Empire balls surround both circular glasses, carved gilt leaves effect a bracket; white painted dial, unique looped hands, Roman chapters, time only. **(A)**

Old Sturbridge Village, Inc.

9-3 Girandole Timepiece
Lemuel Curtis
Concord, MA, c. 1818
H. 39 ", W. 13 "

Empire period, Hepplewhite and French influences, gilded case with painted glass panel connecting upper balloon to lower balloon, painted allegorical scene on lower balloon, gilt balls surround lower balloon, gilt eagle on plinth at top, brass side arms; 8-day movement; white painted dial, Roman chapters, time only. **(A)**

9-4 Girandole Timepiece
Lemuel Curtis
Concord, MA, c. 1820
H. 44 ", W. 15 "

Empire period, classical influence, gilded wood case with curved carved wood sides replacing usual side brass brackets, painted glass tablet and glass in lower balloon-shaped portion, gilt balls surround lower balloon, simulated carved bracket at bottom, eagle on top; 8-day movement, anchor-recoil escapement, pendulum hangs from front plate; white painted dial, diamond-shaped hands, Arabic chapters, time only. **(A)**

9-5 Girandole Timepiece
Lemuel Curtis
Concord, MA, 1820-25
H. 45 ", W. 12 "

Empire period, classical influence, gilded wood case with painted glass panel, "Battle of Lake Erie" painted on convex glass in lower balloon form, Empire gilt balls decorate top and bottom balloons, eagle on ball stands above dial; brass brackets on sides; white painted dial, looped hands effecting a double serpentine design, Roman chapters, time only. "L. CURTIS" inscribed in case panel and stamped on brass works. **(A)**

Israel Sack, Inc., N.Y.C.

10 | Looking Glass Clocks

Despite the fact that clock collectors today associate the looking glass clock with the name of Chauncey Jerome and with his famous stenciled "bronze looking glass" shelf clock, it was Joseph Ives of Bristol, Connecticut, who first housed iron and brass clocks in large looking glass clock cases and who applied for the patent in 1817 to protect the new looking glass door improvement. Since case style was increasingly important to patrons, it was not unusual for the case as well as the movement to have been patented. The idea of a looking glass case was not altogether new to Ives either, according to modern researchers. A letter from Aaron Willard, Jr. to Samuel Terry in 1830 pointed out that Willard and others had, over a twenty-five-year period, occasionally put looking glasses into the fronts of their clocks and timepieces.

The "mirror clock," as we know it today, was particularly popular in Connecticut and New Hampshire in the 1820s and 30s. The frames came in pilaster and scroll designs or as half-round stenciled and gilded columns. The New Hampshire models were compact but relatively expensive, having cases that were large—three to three and one-half feet high—and usually holding eight-day weight-powered metal movements.

10-0 Looking Glass Timepiece (color plate)
Joseph Chadwick
Boscowen, NH, c. 1830
H. 30½", W. 14½", D. 3½"

Empire period, painted and gilt case with turned and ringed half columns on four sides joined by architectural discs at each corner; dial surrounded by black and gilt flowers painted on glass; lower two-thirds is mirror; 8-day weight-driven brass "wheel-barrow" movement, off-center pendulum; white painted dial, Roman chapters, time only. On center dial "Jos. Chadwick Boscowen." **(D)**

Shelburne Museum, Inc.

10-1 Looking Glass Timepiece
James Cary (also Carey)
Brunswick, ME, c. 1815
H. 44", W. 25", D. 8¾"

Empire period, Roman architectural influence, gilded wooden case with engaged columns and American eagle and shield designs on columns, sanded, gilt designed inner frame liner, oak leaves painted around dial on upper glass panels; 8-day weight-driven movement, banjo-style pendulum; white painted concave or "dish" dial, Roman chapters, time only. On dial "James Cary, Brunswick." **(D)**

W. G. Harding

10-2 Looking Glass Clock
"Connecticut Mirror"
Merriman & Birge
Bristol, CT, c. 1818
H. 56", W. 19"

Empire period, Hepplewhite influence, tiger maple and mahogany case with broken arch, brass urn finials, and reeded pilasters, large center mirror panel, top and bottom glass panels painted with landscapes; 8-day iron weight-driven movement; white painted dial, Roman chapters, time and strike. **(D)**

Robert W. Skinner, Inc.

10-3 Looking Glass Clock
Merriman & Ives
Bristol, CT, c. 1820
H. 55", W. 19¼"

Empire period, Hepplewhite influence, mahogany case, reeded pilasters and ionic capitals flanking mirror door, pillar and scroll top with brass urn finials; unlike New Hampshire mirror clocks this one contains square dial like many of the Connecticut, New York and Massachusetts looking glass clocks; white painted dial with scrolls in spandrel corners, Roman chapters, time and strike. **(D)**

Sotheby Parke Bernet

10-4 Looking Glass Timepiece
William Cummens
Roxbury, MA, c. 1830
H. 33¾", W. 15¾"

Empire period, gilded case with half-round engaged columns on all four sides, glass around dial painted black and gold, alarm bell mounted outside on top of case, mirror panel, right lower pillar grooved to allow main wheel to turn; 8-day movement; white painted wood dial, separate second hand and dial in center, Arabic numerals, time and alarm. **(D)**

10-5 Looking Glass Clock
William Emerson
Newport, ME, c. 1830
H. 31", W. 15"

Empire period, gilded frame with half-round engaged columns on all four sides, rosettes carved in four corners, gilded door, mirror panel; 8-day brass movement; white painted dial, Roman chapters, time and strike. **(D)**

10-6 Looking Glass Timepiece
Benjamin Morrill
Boscawen, NH, c. 1830
H. 30″, W. 14½″, D. 4″

Empire period, stenciled glass and wood case, top section with clear glass circle to expose face, green and gold leaves, mirrored lower panel, half-round engaged turned columns on four sides; one weight movement; white painted dial, Roman chapters, time only. **(D)**

10-7 Looking Glass Timepiece
L. W. Noyes
Nashua, NH, c. 1835
H. 30″, W. 14¼″

Empire period, mahogany veneer case, painted black, red, and gilt around dial, mirror panel; 8-day movement; white painted iron dial, Roman chapters, time only. On dial "Warranted by L. W. Noyes." **(D)**

10-8 Looking Glass Clock
Attributed to James Collins
Goffstown, NH, c. 1840
H. 28″, W. 12½″, D. 3¾″

Empire period, gilded frame case with engaged turned columns, flat cornice, red and green paint on upper glass, looking glass on lower panel; 8-day brass weight-driven movement; dial removed to show movement; time and strike. **(D)**

11 | Lyre Timepieces

As far as one can tell, Aaron Willard, Jr., working in the Boston area between 1809 and 1844, invented the **hanging** lyre timepiece. The lyre design, a hallmark of the Empire style, was used on the Continent in clocks that rested on tables and provided an elaborate case variation of the American banjo and the English and French balloon clocks. The inspirations of the Adam brothers, Thomas Hepplewhite, and Thomas Sheraton were reinterpreted and introduced into America by Duncan Phyfe of New York, who has been called the father of the American Empire style. Sketches and prices of Phyfe's lyre-back chairs, dating from about 1815, predated the lyre timepiece design by eight or ten years.

Like the chair, the lyre timepiece is sleek but well carved. Its curvilinear design reflects the new "antique taste" of its period. Empire-style acanthus leaves form the voluptuous base without sacrificing the simple Federal lines of the of the upper case. The glass panels of lyre timepieces retain the classicism of the Federal period in such painted mythological figures as Aurora. Center gilt columns and colorful geometric designs are also classically inspired. A less characteristic lyre was created out of a finished solid-wood panel with fine grain as ornament instead of glass and paint. Among those who executed the solid-wood masterpieces were Aaron Willard, Jr., and John Sawin of Boston, the latter using the carver John Lemon of Salem, Massachusetts.

The first American lyre timepieces and clocks were produced largely in Massachusetts, particularly in the Boston area. Some were made in New Hampshire by Abiel Chandler and in Connecticut by Joseph Ives and J. C. Brown. Ive's creation, with a wooden dial and a square dial frame, was gilded from head to base. Brown's model resembled a stylized figure eight since it had no rectangular base and the squareness of its dial was broken and softened by a curved wood surround. The Ives and Brown models were made for customers by special order.

The "Connecticut lyre," made by the Forestville Manufacturing Company and called by scholars Brooks Palmer and Willis Milham a "wall acorn" timepiece, has a scrolled frame around a square dial plate which vaguely resembles an acorn and vaguely resembles a lyre clock. The rectangular base or pedestal shape of the Willard lyre was replaced by a small, stylized drop form.

11-O Lyre Clock (color plate)
Aaron Willard
Boston, MA, c. 1825-35
H. 38½ ", W. 12¼ "

Empire period, Roman influence, carved and gilded case with leaf and scrolls forming body of lyre; gilded cone finial on plinth above dial; typical Empire gilt balls below base glass which has painted eagle, shield, and flags on white background; white painted dial, Roman chapters, time, strike, and alarm. On dial "Aaron Willard, Boston." **(A)**

Israel Sack, Inc., N.Y.C.

11-1 Lyre Timepiece
Probably a Willard family member
Massachusetts, c. 1825
H. 37"

Empire period, classical influence, mahogany case, brass bezel, convex dial glass, anthemion leaf carving forming base of lyre, tablet depicts naval battle; 8-day weight-driven brass movement; white painted dial, Roman chapters, time only. On glass "Willard's Patent." **(D)**

Robert W. Skinner, Inc.

11-2 Lyre Clock
Lemuel Curtis
Concord, MA, c. 1820-30
H. 39", W. 11", D. 5"

Empire period, Roman influence, mahogany case with painted glass panels, fluted pilaster rising from between two scrolls forming lower curve of lyre, acanthus leaves carved on sides, bold molded base, bracket-type acorn below; white painted dial, brass alarm ring in center of dial, exposed bell, Roman chapters, time, strike, and alarm. On dial "Warranted by L. Curtis." **(A)**

Israel Sack, Inc., N.Y.C.

11-3 Lyre Timepiece
"Connecticut Wall Lyre" and
"Acorn"
Sawin & Dyer (also Dyar)
Boston, MA, c. 1825
H. 44"

Empire period, Roman influence, carved mahogany case with carved spread eagle finial on ball, brass bezel, American shield painted on glass tablet, concealed hinged door in widest curved segment of base section providing access to pendulum; white painted dial, Roman chapters, time only. On dial "Sawin & Dyer/Boston." **(D)**

W.G. Harding

11-4 Lyre Timepiece
"Connecticut Wall Lyre" and
"Acorn"
Aaron Willard, Jr.
Boston, MA, c. 1825
H. 39"

Empire period, Roman influence, mahogany lyre-banjo case with finely-grained mahogany panels at waist and bottom sections, acorn finial on raised plinth, bracket-like base; 8-day movement; white painted dial, spear hands, Roman chapters, time only. **(D)**

W. G. Harding

11-5 Lyre Clock
Joseph Ives
Bristol, CT, c. 1830
H. 34¾", W. 15½"

Empire period, classical influence, gilt carved acanthus leaf lyre case resting on decorated gilt base; 8-day movement; gilded, wooden square dial, frame, and frame liner. Roman chapters, time and strike. Square-faced lyre was not a production model. **(C)**

11-6 Lyre Timepiece
Joshua Seward
Boston, MA, c. 1835
H. 37¼", W. 11¼"

Empire period, classical influence, carved and gilded case, reverse paintings on upper and lower tablets, brass bezel, gilt eagle and ball on plinth at top; white painted dial, Roman chapters, time only. **(D)**

11-7 Lyre Clock
Abiel Chandler
Concord, NH, c. 1835
H. 37¼", W. 11¼"

Empire period, classical influence, all-wood case with carved acanthus leaves ending in scrolls to form the wide lower curve of case, Prince of Wales carved finial on top; 8-day movement, main wheel on strike side is also designed as strike count; white painted dial, Roman chapters, time and strike. **(D)**

11-8 Lyre Clock
"Connecticut Wall Lyre" and "Acorn"
J. C. Brown, Forestville Manufacturing Company
Bristol, CT, c. 1850
H. 36"

Victorian period, classical influence, crotch mahogany veneer case with suggestion of a bracket design supporting lyre; 8-day movement; white painted dial, Roman chapters, time and strike. **(C)**

American Clock & Watch Museum

11-9 Lyre Timepiece
Forestville Manufacturing Company
Forestville, CT, c. 1850
H. 26½", W. 13"

Victorian period, French influence, mahogany veneer case, painted glass tablet with female figure painted in center; 8 day movement; white painted dial, Roman chapters, time only. **(C)**

12 | Schoolhouse Clocks

As early as 1714 English clockmakers had designed an octagonal or round-cornered eight-sided wooden hanging timekeeper with a short case drop which looked very much like what is known today as the schoolhouse clock. The American form, coming in the middle of the next century, continued the simple round or octagonal dial frame and a short twelve-inch drop with its own typical two- or three-sided base. Although twentieth-century clock collectors have been accustomed to making a connection between this short-drop wall clock and the schoolroom, the clock has also hung in post offices, shops, and even saloons. Since Chauncey Jerome referred to it in his catalogue of 1852 as the "octagon eight day" clock and in his circulars prepared for the English market as a "42 inch dial" clock, the term "schoolhouse" must have gained popular recognition much later in the century. Housing wagon or lever spring and other quality spring movements, and often including a separate calendar mechanism, the schoolhouse clock has served as a useful and accurate public timekeeper in a case which still appeals to the modern eye.

A unique schoolhouse variation surfaces in the nineteenth-century barber shop, where an advertisement for a manufacturing company or the name of a retail store might be placed in the center of the dial and where the numerals were painted on backwards for the convenience of men sitting in the barber's chair.

The collector should be aware that the schoolhouse clock was frequently made with cheap and poor movements, as well as with fine mechanisms. Even the term "Regulator" has sometimes been found painted on the glass panel to suggest a precision and quality which are not necessarily integral to the short drop schoolhouse case.

12-O Schoolhouse Timepiece (color plate)
"Lyric," "Drop Octagon"
The E. Ingraham Company
Bristol, CT, c. 1904
H. 25 ", W. 17½ ", D. 3½ ", Dial 13 "

Modern period, Queen Anne influence, press-molded oak octagonal frame and short drop case, metal bezel; 8-day brass movement; white paper dial, Roman chapters, outside calendar ring in Arabic numerals, time only. On dial "Made by The E. Ingraham Co., Bristol, Conn., U.S.A." On glass tablet "Regulator B" [not true regulator]. Listed in 1904 catalogue for $5.85. **(F)**

NAWCCM, Inc.

12-1 Schoolhouse Timepiece
"Drop Octagon" or "Drop Dial"
Joseph Ives
Brooklyn, NY, c. 1850
H. 25 ", W. 17 ", D. 4 "

Victorian period, classical and
Empire influences, octagon rosewood veneer frame and drop;
30-day wagon spring; Roman
chapters, time only. **(A)**

Shelburne Museum, Inc.

12-2 Schoolhouse Clock
E. N. Welch Manufacturing
** Company**
Forestville, CT, c. 1850
H. 18½ ", D. 12 ", Dial 8 "

Victorian period, classical and
Empire influences, molded rosewood octagon dial frame and
drop, brass bezel, gilded horse in
drop glass; 8-day spring driven
mechanism; calendar-incorpo-
rated single dial with calendar
hand, white painted tin dial,
Roman chapters for time, Arabic
numerals for calendar; time,
strike, and day. On back "8 Day/
Axtell/Made by the/E. N. Welch
Mfg. Co./Forestville, Conn. U.S.A."
(F)

Private Collection

12-3 Schoolhouse Clock
"Short Drop"
W. L. Gilbert and Company, manufacturer
Galusha Maranville, patentee
Winchester, CT, c. 1861
H. 25 ", W. 17 "

Victorian period, mahogany veneer octagonal dial frame with short
drop, black and gilt painted on lower glass tablet; 8-day movement;
white painted metal dial, Roman chapters for time, Arabic numerals
on outer dial for days of month, inner dial for days of week, month
opening at top of dial, separate day hand, time and strike. On dial,
"Patented by Galusha Maranville, March 5, 1861." **(F)**

12-4 Schoolhouse Clock
Maker unknown
Probably American, c. 1880
H. 30 "

Victorian period, classical influence, walnut veneer and inlaid round dial frame and drop with small wood side brackets and painted glass lower panel; white painted dial, Roman chapters, time and strike. **(F)**

B.C. & R. Roan, Inc.

12-5 Schoolhouse Timepiece
"Drop Octagon"
Seth Thomas Clock Company
Thomaston, CT, c. 1884
H. 23¹⁹⁄₁₆ ", W. 16⅛ "

Victorian period, classical influence, octagonal wood dial frame and drop, painted glass lower panel and oval for pendulum bob; white painted dial, Roman chapters, time only. On dial "Seth Thomas." **(F)**

The National Museum of History and Technology, Smithsonian Institution

12-6 Schoolhouse Timepiece
"Drop Octagon" or "Drop Dial"
Seth Thomas Clock Company
Thomaston, CT, c. 1884
H. 23 ", W. 16 "

Victorian period, classical influence, octagonal wood dial frame and drop; black and gilt painted lower glass panel with oval for pendulum bob; calendar incorporated in single dial, white painted dial, second hand, Roman chapters, time and day. On dial "Seth Thomas/Made in U.S.A." **(F)**

B.C. & R. Roan, Inc.

12-7 Schoolhouse Timepiece
Seth Thomas Clock Company
Thomaston, CT, c. 1884
H. 18"

Victorian period, classical influence, laminated oak circular dial frame and drop, round glass to see pendulum bob; white painted dial, Arabic chapters, time only. On dial "Seth Thomas/Made in U.S.A." **(F)**

B.C. & R. Roan, Inc.

12.8 Schoolhouse Clock
"Anglo-American Schoolhouse"
W. Gibson, manufacturer or retailer
New Haven Clock Company, movement maker
England and New Haven, CT, c. 1890
H. 32", W. 18"

Victorian period, long drop, double scroll case with wood marquetry; 8-day movement; white painted dial, Roman chapters, time and strike. On dial: "W. Gibson—Appleby." Inscribed on movement: "New Haven Clock Co., U.S.A." **(F)**

Lorretta Marder Interiors

12-9 Schoolhouse Clock
Waterbury Clock Company
Waterbury, CT, c. 1895
Dial 12"

Victorian period, classical influence, oak veneer case, octagonal dial frame and short drop with clear glass pendulum bob oval; 8-day movement; white painted dial, Roman chapters, time and strike. Listed in 1895 Sears, Roebuck & Company catalogue for $3.95. **(F)**

**12-10 Schoolhouse Timepiece
"Alba"**
Seth Thomas Clock Company
Thomaston, CT, c. 1928
H. 18 ", W. 11½ ", D. 3½ "

Modern period, classical influence, round oak short-drop case, brass bezel, round pendulum bob glass; 8-day pendulum movement No. 41; white painted dial, Arabic chapters, spade hands, time only. **(F)**

NAWCCM, Inc.

13 | Calendar Clocks (Wall)

Given a radio, a desk calendar, and an electric clock, we tend to take time and date for granted in the twentieth century. Before 1870 and the adoption of Standard Time, however, such was hardly the case. Although there had obviously long existed calendar mechanisms in clocks—the simple calendar attachments in many grandfather clocks being a particular case in point—the perfection of a separate calendar clock mechanism in the mid-nineteenth century, a movement sufficiently inexpensive to be acquired by the average man, was a continuation of the technological trend of miniaturization that is a prime characteristic of nineteenth-century industry.

By 1860, and for very little more than the cost of a plain wall or shelf clock, the middle-class man could own a calendar clock of his own. He could buy it in a decorative double-dial "Ionic" model or in the "peanut" or "figure-eight" shapes. He could also purchase a single-dial timekeeper with an extra hand and two sets of numbers, one outside the other. The Arabic numerals on the outside recorded the date; the Roman chapters on the inside recorded the time.

Calendar clocks, like most other timekeepers, exhibit the features of the prevailing furniture styles of their day. Through the years they were designed with flat tops, Queen Anne arched heads, Chippendale scrolls, architectural or Baroque pediments, and modified and sharp Gothic tops; they appeared as well in gingerbread cabinets of the late nineteenth century and in the Mission oak cases of the early twentieth. Like the innovative furniture of these same periods, they were made of cast iron, pressed papier mâché, and ceramics as well as of traditional wood. They included both time and time-and-strike movements. Of the few specialized makers of nineteenth-century calendar movements, the Ithaca Clock Company of New York was the most successful.

13-O Calendar Timepiece (color plate)
Ithaca Calendar Clock Company, manufacturer
J. S. Reynolds Foundry, iron case
H. B. Horton, inventor
L. Hubbell, maker of brass movement
Ithaca, NY, c. 1866
H. 21", W. 9¼", D. 3½"

Victorian period, French influence, iron case painted black with strawberries and leaves painted in center, brass bezels; 30-day two-spring pendulum movement; upper dial paper, Roman chapters, moon shaped hands, time only even though it has two wind squares; lower paper dial Arabic numerals, day, date and month. On lower dial "H. B. Horton's/ Patents/Calendar/Ap! 18th, 1865/and/Au9 28th, 1866/Ithaca Calendar Clock Company/Ithaca, N.Y." **(D)**

NAWCCM, Inc.

13-1 Calendar Timepiece
Seth Thomas
Plymouth Hollow, CT, c. 1865
H. 40½", W. 19", D. 6½"

Victorian period, wood case, lower dial with Arabic numerals shows date, day, and month; 8-day striking movement; white painted upper dial, Roman chapters, time only. On upper dial "Regulator." On lower dial "Calendar/Seth Thomas Clock Co." Patent dates from Sept. 14, 1854 to March 4, 1862. **(D)**

**13-2 Calendar Timepiece
"No. 4 Office Clock"
Ithaca Calendar Clock Company, manufacturer
E. N. Welch, movement maker
H. B. Horton, calendar movement maker
Ithaca, NY; Bristol, CT, c. 1875
H. 29", W. 16", D. 4½"**

Victorian period, classical influence, oak double-dial case; 30-day brass movement, two mainsprings showing two wind squares, though it is only a timepiece, nickel plated pendulum bob; upper dial removed to show mechanism; white painted lower dial, time only; day, date and month on upper dial. On lower dial "Ithaca Calendar Clock Co./ Ithaca, N.Y." A variation priced at $16.00 is in the 1880 catalogue. **(D)**

NAWCCM, Inc.

**13-3 Calendar Clock
"Gale Astronomical Calendar Clock"
Daniel Jackson Gale, calendar movement maker
Welch, Spring & Company, movement maker
Bristol, CT; Forestville, CT, c. 1880
H. 31", W. 16½", D. 4"**

Victorian period, rosewood and veneer long-drop case, black and gilt glass panel; 8-day brass movement; five dials in one: the large outside in Arabic numerals is the day of the month; small time dial above calendar arbor is in Roman chapters; to right is moon's age dial; to left is day of the week dial; dial below center arbor shows month of the year and day of the month at the end of every seven days; time and strike. **(D)**

NAWCCM, Inc.

**13-4 Calendar Clock
"Ionic"
New Haven Clock Company
New Haven, CT, c. 1880
H. 29", upper dial 12", lower dial 10"**

Victorian period, classical influence, wood frame volutes carved between upper and lower dials; 8-day spring movement; white painted upper dial, Roman chapters, separate day hand, time and strike; white lower dial, Arabic numerals, separate hand for months of the year. **(E)**

13-5 Calendar Clock
Seth Thomas Clock Company
Thomaston, CT, c. 1880
H. 24"

Victorian period, wood case with three turned wood finials, lower dial with Arabic numerals shows date, day, and month; 8-day double spring movement; white painted upper dial, Roman chapters, time and strike. On lower dial "Manufactured by/The Ithaca Clock Co." **(D)**

13-6 Calendar Clock
Ithaca Calendar Clock Co.
Ithaca, NY, c. 1890
H. 36"

Victorian period, Renaissance and Oriental influences, press-molded wood with incised design on case and pendulum bob, pendulum hangs in front of calendar dial, fretwork top; white painted upper dial with Roman chapters, time and strike; lower calendar dial with Arabic numerals, day, date, and month. On dial "H. B. . . . Patent/Ithaca Calendar Clock Co." **(D)**

B. C. & R. Roan, Inc.

13-7 Calendar Clock
Waterbury Clock Co.
Waterbury, CT, c. 1890
H. 29"

Victorian period, Eastlake influence, press-molded case with flat cornice; double decker dials both white with upper dial in Roman chapters, time and strike, and lower dial in Arabic numerals showing day, date, and month. **(D)**

B. C. & R. Roan, Inc.

14 | Figure Eights

Following the progression of design from the straight wall case to the curvilinear, from the Greek line to the Roman curve, from the Willard banjo to the girandole and lyre, the figure eight became one of the most popular designs ever to grace the horological marketplace. Resembling Victorian chair backs and sofa frames, these double balloon shapes housed either fine regulator movements, or separate calendar and time movements. For the buyer with a limited pocketbook, figure eights were also equipped with time mechanisms. Sometimes decorated with volutes or cast metal flowers, they satisfied the popular classical tastes of their day.

Elias Ingraham, a cabinetmaker turned clock manufacturer and known primarily for his cases, designed a wall model he called "Ionic" and which some today call "round drop." Ingraham's figure eight incorporated a set of balloon shapes with volutes separating the balloons; and it housed either a simple eight-day spring movement with the lower balloon as a decorative space for the pendulum, or a timepiece above and a calendar mechanism below. Edward Howard, however, is the most renowned of all the figure-eight model makers. His "figures," made after 1859 when his partner David Porter Davis left the company, were cased in five sizes—numbers six through ten, following the company's tradition of numbering Howard banjos (one though five). According to the Howard catalogue, the largest figure eight—fifty-eight inches high with a fourteen-inch dial and an eight-inch-long pendulum—was number six. The smallest—thirty-three inches high with an eight-inch dial and a three-inch-long pendulum—was number ten.

Unlike the banjos, the Howard figure eights had half-round gilded pendulums. The three smallest sizes had moon-shaped hands; the two largest, diamond-shaped. The volutes at the top and the base of the balloons, like the curve of the black and gilt lines painted on the glass, echo the shape of the round, classical case.

14-O Figure Eight Timepiece (color plate)
"No. 10, House and Counting Room Clock"
E. Howard and Company
Boston, MA, c. 1871
H. 33", W. 11", D. 3¾", Dial 8"

Victorian period, French influence, black walnut case, volute on top and volute at bottom, black paint and gilt on middle glass panel, black, red, and gilt on lower panel, pendulum rod gilded; recoil escapement; white painted metal dial, Roman chapters, moon-shaped hands, time only. On dial "E. Howard & Co./Boston." Same inscription printed on label. **(A)**

Private Collection

14-1 Figure Eight Timepiece
Sometimes called a "Banjo"
Attributed to George D. Hatch
North Attleboro, MA, c. 1860
H. 33", W. 14¼", D. 3¾"

Victorian period, Federal influence, mahogany veneer case,
wood bezel, black and gilt on
both glass panels; 8-day brass
movement, brass pendulum rod;
white painted metal dial, Roman
chapters, moon-shaped hands,
time only.

NAWCCM, Inc.

14-2 Figure Eight Clock
"Ionic Model"
E. Ingraham & Company
Bristol, CT, c. 1861-80
H. 22", W. 14", D. 4", Dial 10"

Victorian period, Federal influence, rosewood and veneer
case, gilt, silver, and black
painted on lower glass tablet,
volutes between separate round
doors; 8-day brass movement;
white painted metal dial, Roman
chapters, moon-shaped hands,
time and strike. On label "E. Ingraham & Co., Bristol, Conn." Patented Dec. 3, 1861. Listed in 1880
catalogue for $8.00 and for $7.00
time only. **(F)**

NAWCCM, Inc.

14-3 Figure Eight Timepiece
"Office No. 1"
Seth Thomas Clock Company
Thomaston, CT, c. 1870
H. 25½", W. 15", D. 3¾"

Victorian period, Federal influence, rosewood veneer case,
black and gilt design on lower
glass tablet, raised wood cones
decorate case, molded wood
bezel; 8-day spring movement;
white paper on metal dial, Arabic
chapters, time only. Label on inside. **(F)**

NAWCCM, Inc.

14-4 Figure Eight Timepiece
E. Howard Clock Company
Boston and Waltham, MA, c. 1872
H. 37¼"

Victorian period, classical influence, walnut case with volutes, one at top and one at bottom, black and gilt painted glass panel; lower balloon has flat circular glass with gold leaf rings; white painted dial, Roman chapters, time only.

E. Howard Clock Company

14-5 Figure Eight Timepiece
"Reflector"
New Haven Clock Company
New Haven, CT, c. 1880
H. 29½", Dial 12"

Victorian period, classical influence, wood case, volutes separate upper and lower balloon shapes; 8-day spring movement; white painted dial, Roman chapters, time only. **(F)**

14-6 Figure Eight Timepiece
"Ionic," "Round Drop"
E. Ingraham & Company
Bristol, CT, c. 1884
H. 22", Diam. 8"

Victorian period, classical influence, mahogany case with lower glass drop painted showing ship design, two volutes separate the two circles; 8-day movement; white painted dial, Roman chapters, time only. Patented Oct. 8, 1872 and Nov. 4, 1873. **(F)**

Robert W. Skinner, Inc.

**14-7 Figure Eight Variation
"Ramona"
Sessions Clock Company
Forestville, CT, 1906-20
H. 29½", W. 14¼", D. 4½"**

Modern period, Mission style,
stained oak case with lower clear
glass tablet; 8-day brass movement; wood dial with metal Arabic
chapters, spade hands, time only.
(F)

NAWCCM, Inc.

15 | Cuckoo Clocks

The most famous and cherished novelty timekeeper, a rival of the
grandfather clock in popular appeal, was the hanging automated
cuckoo clock, a low-priced German invention. According to most
clock historians, it was first made in the 1730s in the Black Forest by
Franz Anton Kellerer of Schönwald. The source of Kellerer's inspira-
tion was said to have been the rooster atop the famous Strasbourg
Cathedral. He used the call of the cuckoo, however, an easier
sound to imitate than the crow of the rooster.

Cuckoo clocks—wag-on-the-walls with painted dials, wooden
movements, and birds with moveable and sometimes feathered
wings—were certainly imported for sale in America by the end of the
eighteenth century, and it is possible that some were even manufactured in the New World. Americans, however, first developed a
serious affection for the quaint little wall clock when the "railroad at-
tendant" style of its case was fully realized. In its gabled oak Black
Forest case, the late-Victorian householder saw "an Eastlake cottage to shelter the bird," as one critic has noted. By the late nineteenth century, the immense popularity of the cuckoo clock was in
part the result of its "authentic" Old-World charm. Most contemporary manufacturers, in fact, boasted that their cuckoo cases
were of "genuine" Black Forest construct, even if the works themselves were Connecticut-made. For this reason, the collector will
find the **complete** American cuckoo clock (case and movement) a
relative rarity.

15-O Cuckoo Clock (color plate)
American Clock Company
Philadelphia, PA, c. 1930
H. 17", W. 14", D. 7½"

Modern period, Victorian influence, carved wood case, carved spread eagle at top of branches; 8-day brass mass-produced movement, iron pendulum; cuckoo painted red, blue and black, ivory Roman chapters, time only. **(F)**

Shelburne Museum, Inc.

15-1 Cuckoo Clock
Maker unknown
Case probably German; movement probably CT, c. 1910
H. 36"

Modern period, Victorian influence, wood carved case with bird, branches, leaf and fruit design, weights in the form of pine cones; ivory Roman chapters, time and strike. **(F)**

B. C. & R. Roan, Inc.

15-2 Cuckoo Clock
The Lux Clock Manufacturing Company
Waterbury, CT, c. 1917
H. 7½", W. 5½", D. 1½"

Modern period, carved wood, gabled roof, leaves and birds as ornaments, red cuckoo in window above dial; brass spring movement with pendulum; dial has Roman chapters, time and strike. On dial "Lux U.S.A." On back "Lux Clock Mfg. Co. in Waterbury, Conn. U.S. Patents Pending." **(G)**

NAWCCM, Inc.

15-3 Cuckoo Clock
Keebler Clock Company
Philadelphia, PA, c. 1920
H. 5″, W. 4″, D. 1¾″

Modern period, rustic pressed-wood log design with leaves, flowers, buds and nest of birds on boughs; brass spring pendulum movement; dial with Arabic chapters, time and strike. On back "Keebler Clock Co./Philadelphia, Pa./Patents Pending." **(G)**

NAWCCM, Inc.

15-4 Cuckoo Timepiece
"Pendulette"
Lux Clock Manufacturing Company
Waterbury, CT, c. 1930
H. 6½″, W. 3⅞″

Modern period, German influence, gabled house with chimney, trellises and vine climbing sides of case, bird perched over numeral 12; 30-hour spring movement; natural wood dial, Roman chapters, time only. **(G)**

16 | Wall Novelties

The innovative designs and technological advancements of the nineteenth century were certainly responsible for much of the novel and special productions one sees in the clocks of that century. But perhaps a growing desire for light amusement, expressed at the end of the eighteenth century in Simon Willard's "gravity clock," evinced a new freedom, a winding-down of puritanical restraint to say, "Let me play; let me make amusing things."

The Victorians and their immediate successors were particularly fond of yoking unlike objects, and clocks were frequently housed in all types of unlikely cases—cast-iron tree trunks, brass wheelbarrows, porcelain puppy dogs. But whether or not one thinks of these forms as kitsch, the iron skillet timepiece, the porcelain plate clock, and the Dickory Dickory Docks were "fun things" for adults to observe and to enjoy. Special clocks, like the Columbus and patriotic timepieces, symbolized nostalgic moments for American citizens—the cherished discovery of America, the adoption of the shield and stars to represent the new nation. Other specialties, like the marine or ship's bell clock, so necessary in the twentieth century, had innovative movements which could work well at sea and ring the hours in Navy time. Here utility, as in the gaslight arm clock, overrides both sentiment and playful bad taste.

16-O Specialty (color plate)
"Patriotic Gallery Timepiece," "Navy"
Jerome and Company
Bristol, CT, c. 1852
H. 20", W. 15½", D. 3¾", Dial 9"

Victorian period, Federal motifs, papier mache case, mother-of-pearl inlay; 8-day brass movement; white painted dial, Roman chapters, time only. **(E)**

NAWCCM, Inc.

16-1 Specialty
"Gravity" Timepiece
Simon Willard
MA, c. 1795-1800
H. 26¾", Base H. 10⅞", W. 8½"

Federal period, mahogany case surmounted by brass spread eagle; bell exposed, brass pendulum, steel bell, 4-day movement; brass dial, Roman chapters, time only. On dial "Simon Willard Inv't & Fecit for Mr. & Mrs. R. Brown.

Shelburne Museum, Inc.

16-2 Specialty
"Plate Clock"
Ansonia Clock Company
New York, NY, c. 1890
Diam. 14"

Victorian period, brass embossed plate; 8-day movement; porcelain dial, Roman chapters, time only. Inscribed on movement: "Ansonia Clock Co., U.S.A." **(F)**

Lorretta Marder Interiors

16-3 Novelty
"Columbus Timepiece"
Bostwick & Burgess Manufacturing Company
Norwalk, OH, c. 1893
H. 14", W. 5½", D. 5⅛"

Victorian period, souvenir made for the Columbian Exhibition of 1893; wood construction with profile of Columbus at top and "1492" impressed below dial, two acorn drops hang from foliot; pinwheel escapement; wood dial, Arabic chapters, time only. In 1894 Columbus clocks were distributed by two New York City theaters as prizes. **(G)**

B. C. & R. Roan, Inc.

16-4 Specialty
"Ship's Bell," "Marine," "Wardroom Clock"
Maker unknown
Portsmith, NH, c. 1900
Diam. 15¼"

Victorian period, circular molded mahogany case and hinged bezel; marine movement; silvered dial, slow-fast mechanism, separate second hand and dial, Arabic numerals, time and strike. On dial "Ham's Ship Bell." **(E)**

Sotheby Parke Bernet

16-5 - Novelty
"Plate Clock"
Maker unknown
Place unknown, c. 1910
Diam. of dial 11"

Modern period, blue and white ceramic plate, velvet frame wood box for movement on back; spring movement; dial has Arabic chapters, spade hands, time only. **(G)**

NAWCCM, Inc.

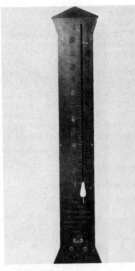

16-6 Novelty
"Mouse Clock" or "Dickory
  Dickory Dock"
Dungan & Klump
Philadelphia, PA, c. 1910
H. 43½ "

Modern period, pine case painted black; raised metal numbers, wooden mouse with leather tail; 1-day brass spring movement; slow-fast mechanism; applied metal Arabic numerals. On case "No. 912833/Pat. Feb. 16, 1909." **(F)**

NAWCCM, Inc.

16-7 Specialty
"Marine Timepiece"
Chelsea Clock Company
Boston, MA, c. 1911
Diam. 7⅛ "

Modern period, round brass case with screw bezel; 8-day balance-wheel movement; black dial with white Arabic chapters, separate second hand and dial, seconds bit, time only. Price in 1911 $33.00. On dial "U. S. NAVY/DECK CLOCK NO. 3."

W. G. Harding

16-8 Novelty
"Gaslight Arm Timepiece"
Crescent Watch Case Company
Newark, NJ, c. 1923
Diam. of dial 5 ", arm 19 "

Modern period, metal case, bezel, and arm; porcelain dial illuminated by gas, spade hands, Arabic chapters, time only. Illustration shows clock and arm unattached. **(G)**

NAWCCM, Inc.

16-9 Specialty
"House Clock"
Seth Thomas Clock Company
Thomaston, CT, c. 1895
H. 26", W. 11"

Victorian period, fruitwood case, brass bezel, levers and card holders; white, porcelain dial, Roman chapters, time and strike. Unusual "Upstairs-Downstairs" timepiece electrified to send signals to domestic help in separate part of house. Painted on dial and engraved on movement: "Seth Thomas." **(G)**

Lorretta Marder Interiors

17 | Advertising Clocks

Men named Baird, Gilbert, Sessions, and Sidney—clockmakers, all—produced timekeepers for use in the new world of nineteenth-century advertising. On their clocks they promoted liniments for the skin, tanner's oil for leather goods, Calumet Baking Powder, and other commercial products. In 1886 the Sidney Advertising Clock Company of New York patented an eight-day brass movement with a cam triggering a separate movement in the clock base which turned the drums placed at the bottom of each case and released a succession of ads once every five minutes.

A few advertising clocks, like those of Edward P. Baird of Plattsburg, New York, simply applied the manufacturer's name and the name of the product, or the advertiser's slogan to the case.

17-O Advertising Timepiece (color plate)
Gilbert Clock Company
Winsted, CT, c. 1905
H. 40", W. 14½", D. 4½"

Modern period, pine case, flat cornice, advertisement painted on lower glass tablet in gilt, green, red, and silver; 8-day "stretch" version of 38" "Washington" model, A-frame movement, brass bushed steel plates; white, paper on tin dial, Arabic chapters, spade hands, time only. On dial "Gilbert." On glass "Sauer's/Flavoring/Best by/Every Test/Extracts." **(E)**

NAWCCM, Inc.

17-1 Advertising Timepiece Sidney Advertising Clock Company
Sidney, NY, c. 1890
H. 68½", W. 28", D. 10¼

Victorian period, black painted wood case with architectural top, turned wood finials, stylized center arch, four bracket ornaments below cornice, lower case with three cylindrical cases for ads, voluted bracket below case; brass movement with cam which causes a separate movement to release every five minutes and show three different ads; four ads on each of three drums, 8-day run; white, painted metal dial, Roman chapters for time, Arabic numerals outside ring for day calendar, separate red calendar hand, time only. On dial "TIME." On glass tablet "Advertisements [Change] Every 5 Minutes." Patented July 20, 1886 **(D)**

NAWCCM, Inc.

17-2 Advertising Timepiece Edward P. Baird Clock Company Plattsburgh, NY, c. 1895
H. 30½", W. 18½", D. 4"

Victorian period, red and silver painted, wood case, variation of Seth Thomas No. 97 movement, 36-tooth escape wheel; white paper dial, Roman chapters, time only. On frame of case "Vanner & Prest's 'molliscorium' [oil for softening harness leathers], Compo. V P trademark Embrocation" [the former used by curriers and tanners, the latter a liniment for human beings]. On movement "Baird Clock Co./Plattsburgh/NY" and "15." On dial "Seth Thomas Movement/Edw. P. Baird & Co./Plattsburgh, NY **(E)**

NAWCCM, Inc.

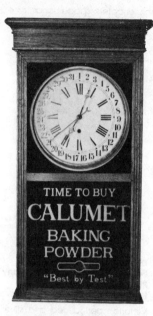

17-3 Advertising Timepiece "Regulator No. 2" (not true regulator)
Sessions Clock Company
Bristol, CT, c. 1904
H. 33¾", W. 18", D. 4¾"

Modern period, stained oak case, reeded door, black paint and gilt on upper and lower glass tablets; 8-day brass spring movement, wood pendulum rod, brass bob; white paper dial on tin, Roman chapters and Arabic calendar rings, separate red second hand, time with calendar. On dial "Made by the Sessions Clock Co., Forestville, Conn. U.S.A." On Tablet "Time to Buy/CALUMET/Baking Powder/'Best by Test.'" On label "The Sessions Clock Company Forestville." **(E)**

NAWCCM, Inc.

III SHELF CLOCKS

18 | Bracket Clocks

The name "bracket clock," technically refers to a high-grade movement driven by steel springs and controlled by a fusee and with a short six-inch pendulum. It derives its common name, however, not from its movement, but from the modern observation that the clock could be placed on a wall bracket or shelf. "Bracket" is a misleading and superficial reference, however, since the seventeenth-century table clock, the eighteenth-century chimney or spring clock, and the nineteenth-century mantel clock could each sit on a wall bracket and were, therefore, all candidates for the term "bracket clock." Accurate or not, the name "bracket clock" has stuck and now conjures fine ebony, mahogany, or walnut woods, and a strong resemblance to the hood of a grandfather clock of the early Colonial period, with a Queen Anne-style dome top, arched dial plate, and detailed engraving on both the back and front plates. Very often it has a brass handle at the top, much like the carriage clock, or sometimes two handles, one on each side, which was used to carry it from the parlor to the bedroom where it was most often needed. It usually contained elaborate alarms and repeaters and was an expensive mechanism, cost and steel springs limiting its production in Colonial and Federal America. Only in style centers, port cities, and inland wagon road towns like Boston, Philadelphia, Charleston, South Carolina, and Lancaster, Pennsylvania, was there support for the few American makers of the bracket clock form.

18-0 Bracket Clock (color plate)
F. Heisely
Harrisburg, PA, c. 1820
H. 20½ ", W. 16½ ", D. 7¼ "

Empire period, Queen Anne and Hepplewhite influences, cherry case, arched head and dial, Hepplewhite feet; white painted dial with flowers in spandrel corners and larger flowers painted in arch above dial, Arabic chapters, time and strike. On dial "F. Heisely. Harrisburg."
(D)

William Penn Memorial Museum, Pennsylvania Historical and Museum Commission

18-1 Bracket Clock
William Lee
Charleston, SC, c. 1750-70
H. 16½ ", W. 9¾ ", D. 7 "

Colonial period, Queen Anne influence, ebonized mahogany case, domed top with a brass bail handle above a molded cornice; brass short bob pendulum movement, pull repeater; brass arched dial with brass spandrels in four corners and in arch above dial, Roman chapters, time and repeater. **(C)**

18-2 Bracket Clock
Joseph Pearsall
New York, NY, c. 1774
H. 22 "

Colonial period, Queen Anne influence, ebonized pine case, dome top with brass handle; 8-day spring fusee brass movement with crown wheel escapement; brass dial with brass spandrels in corners and above in arch, separate second hand and dial in arch, Roman chapters, date on lower dial, time and strike. On dial "Joseph Pearsall New York." **(C)**

18-3 Bracket Clock
Charles Geddes
New York, NY, c. 1775
H. 17½", W. 10¼", D. 6¾"

Colonial period, Queen Anne influence, walnut case, dome top with brass handle; brass dial and spandrels, day calendar opening, separate second dial and hand, Roman chapters, time and silent strike. On dial "Chas Geddes New York." **(C)**

Israel Sack, Inc., N.Y.C.

18-4 Bracket Clock
Thomas Parker
Philadelphia, PA, c. 1790
H. 14½", W. 11", D. 7¾"

Federal period, Queen Anne and Chippendale influences, ebonized case with brass handle and ogee bracket feet; 8-day fusee movement; engraved brass arched dial, Roman chapters, time and strike. **(D)**

W.G. Harding

18-5 Bracket Clock
John Child
Philadelphia, PA, c. 1835
H. 16 ", W. 11 ", D. 7½ "

Empire period, Queen Anne influence, cherry and veneer case with Queen Anne arch and Hepplewhite glass oval on the side, ball feet, brass handles on sides; white painted dial with flowers painted in spandrel corners, separate second hand and dial, Roman chapters, time and strike. On dial "John Child Philad?" **(D)**

Index of American Design, National Gallery of Art, Washington

19 | Massachusetts Shelf Clocks

The Massachusetts shelf clock, a popular and modern name for a specific timekeeping design which looked like a case on a case, or a case on a bracket, came on the market about 1790. According to one historian, it used less brass than tall-case clocks; its production was, therefore, less costly; it housed improved precision movements; it rivaled the expensive and elegant bracket clock popular in England and America among people of good taste. Although on first glance it resembled the grandmother clock, with height measurements of thirty-one inches to thirty-eight inches, the proportions were very different. It was all head and base and had no visible pendulum case joining together the top with the bottom.

This clock form, alternately called a "box-on-box," "case-on-case," "half-shelf," and "thirty-hour," was first designed in Massachusetts, presumably by the famous Willard family. In addition to Aaron Willard, there were at least four other clockmakers who produced the Massachusetts shelf—David Wood, Daniel Balch, Joseph Loring, and John Sawin. Levi Hutchins, William Fitz, Silas Parsons, and Benjamin Morrill of New Hampshire and Nathan Hale of Vermont were among those from other states to copy the original Willard model.

Simon Willard's shelf movement is very much like his banjo mechanism. Both feature eight-day movements and tend to be timepieces rather than clocks. Those of Balch and Aaron Willard are thirty-hour clocks. When smaller weights were introduced, the shelf clock was often wound with a key instead of by pulling on the chain and weight every thirty hours. Architectural pediments and ogee bracket feet are characteristic touches of the Colonial and Chippendale taste carried into the early Federal period. French splay feet and kidney- or balloon-shaped dial plates, however, express the true Federal taste in Massachusetts shelf clocks. Those made in the Empire period display brass or gilt ball feet and a flat or simplified scroll top.

19-0 Massachusetts Shelf Timepiece (color plate)
Aaron Willard
Boston, MA, c. 1780
H. 30", W. 12", D. 6"

Federal period, Chippendale and Hepplewhite influences, walnut case, pastoral scene painted on lower wood panel attributed to John Ritto Penniman, brass urn-shaped finials, stylized bracket feet; 8-day movement with anchor-recoil escapement and half second pendulum same as used in Banjo clocks except that weight falls in front of pendulum; kidney-shaped dial plate, red flowers painted below dial, Roman chapters, time only. **(A)**

Private Collection

19-1 Massachusetts Shelf Timepiece
William Fitz
Portsmouth, NH, c. 1760-80
H. 27¼", W. 11½"

Colonial period, Chippendale influence, mahogany case with fluted pilasters on lower half of case, scrolls and single brass urn-shaped finial on top of upper case; weight-driven movement; brass dial, Roman chapters, time only. Called Massachusetts shelf timepiece because of case style though movement was made in New Hampshire; cases were probably made by one cabinetmaker in Massachusetts. On dial "William Fitz/Portsmith." **(B)**

19-2 Massachusetts Shelf Timepiece
Simon Willard
Roxbury, MA, c. 1770-75
H. 29½", W. 13", D. 4½"

Colonial period, Chippendale influence, mahogany case, unique single urn-shaped, brass finial, appearance of two brass feet on upper part of case, brass rope edge on upper case, kidney-shaped glass panel; brass dial and neck plate, Roman chapters, time only. On neck plate "Simon/Willard/Roxbury." **(A)**

Israel Sack, Inc., N.Y.C.

19-3 Massachusetts Shelf Clock
Daniel Balch, Jr.
Newburyport, MA, c. 1790-1800
H. 28½", W. 12", D. 6"

Federal period, Chippendale influence, mahogany case with two sets of reeded pilasters on lower base (the larger pilasters on corners of case and the inner smaller pilasters on door panel), lower door with keystone and arch, scrolled pediment, plinths hold brass urn and flame finials; brass dial, Roman chapters, time and strike. On dial plate "Dan! Balch, Jr. Newbury Port." **(A)**

Israel Sack, Inc., N.Y.C.

19-4 Massachusetts Shelf Timepiece
Joseph Loring
Sterling, MA, c. 1791-1812
H. 38¾", W. 12¾", D. 6½"

Federal period, Hepplewhite influence, mahogany fan inlay in lower case, dome top with open serpentine fretwork on either side of inlaid plinth holding brass urn finial, French tapered splayed feet inimical to the Hepplewhite style; 8-day movement; white painted kidney-shaped dial plate, Roman chapters, time only. On dial plate "Joseph Loring." **(A)**

Israel Sack, Inc., N.Y.C.

19-5 Massachusetts Shelf Timepiece
David Wood
Newburyport, MA, c. 1800-10
H. 32", W. 11¾", D. 6"

Federal period, Hepplewhite influence, mahogany case inlaid with striated oval spandrels, ogee bracket feet in Chippendale style, wavy pediment, plinths support urn and flame brass finials; white painted dial, Roman chapters, time only. On dial "D. Wood." **(A)**

Private Collection

19-6 Massachusetts Shelf Timepiece
David Wood
Newburyport, MA, c. 1800
H. 36¼", W. 12", D. 5½"

Federal period, Hepplewhite influence; mahogany, satinwood, or birch case with cross-banded and inlaid borders, small quarter column on lower base fluted plinths supporting brass urn finials, solid wood arched top, French tapered feet, oval side handles with masked centers used by Wood on his better clocks; white painted dial, green fans painted in spandrel corners, landscape scene painted in arch on dial, Roman chapters, time only. On dial "David Wood Newburyport." **(A)**

Israel Sack, Inc., N.Y.C.

19-7 Massachusetts Shelf Timepiece
Aaron Willard and William Cummens
Roxbury, MA, c. 1800
H. 35", W. 12½"

Federal period, Hepplewhite influence, mahogany case with open fretwork and three brass urn-shaped finials, the center one on a plinth, kidney-shaped glass in door, French splayed feet; a single train movement; white painted dial, Roman chapters, time only. On dial plate "Aaron Willard, Roxbury/Warranted by/Wm Cummens." On inside of hood "1798 Cummens." **(A)**

19-8 Massachusetts Shelf Clock
Aaron Willard
Boston, MA, c. 1815
H. 35¼", W. 12¼"

Empire period, Sheraton influence, mahogany case, scrolled top with plinth supporting brass ball and spread eagle, brass feet and bold cushion-molded base, female with urn surrounded by flowers painted in lower glass tablet, stylized columns painted in corners; upper tablet also painted with flowers, leaves, and columns; white painted dial, Roman chapters, time and strike. Painted on upper glass "Aaron

Willard/Boston." **(A)**

Sotheby Parke Bernet

19-9 Massachusetts Shelf Timepiece
Aaron Willard
Boston, MA, c. 1815
H. 36", W. 12¼"

Empire period, Hepplewhite influence, mahogany and veneer case, swan's neck scrolls, brass ball finial with spread wing eagle above it, brass paw feet, flowers and oak leaves painted on both glass panels, anchors painted in corner ovals of upper panel; shepherd playing flute, lambs, and house painted on lower panel; white painted dial, Roman chapters, time only. On glass "Aaron Willard,/Boston." **(A)**

Sotheby Parke Bernet

19-10 Massachusetts Shelf Timepiece
John Sawin
Boston, MA, c. 1830
H. 30", W. 13½", Dial 6"

Empire period, Roman influence, wood veneer case, flat top, mirror tablet, painted glass around dial; one train, weight-driven movement; white painted dial, Roman chapters, time only. **(B)**

19-11 Massachusetts Shelf Timepiece
O. Brackett
Vassalboro, ME, c. 1840
H. 28¼", W. 9¼"

Victorian period, cherrywood and maple case, molded cornice and case with molded door; weight-driven movement; white painted dial, Roman chapters, time only. On dial "O. Brackett/Vassalboro." **(C)**

---

20 | Beehive Clocks

The beehive clock, an English Gothic bracket form with a lancet or slightly curved, modified, pointed arch (sometimes called "round Gothic"), was used as early as the thirteenth century. It was popular again in England between 1800 and 1850, and through the work of clockmaker William Thompson it also found favor in Baltimore, Maryland, in 1800.

About 1837 the beehive case reappeared in Connecticut. It housed the first American reverse fusee and spring mechanism which allowed cost and size of clocks to be reduced once again. According to Thomas E. Grimshaw, the fusee was probably invented by Charles Kirk; the spring, by Joseph Shaylor Ives; the case, possibly by Elias Ingraham; and the whole package, manufactured by E. C. Brewster. The flat and inlaid surfaces of Federal design were replaced by bulging, half-round, and sometimes rippled veneer moldings. The dimensional qualities reflect the drama of light and shadow, of lean and round, of chaste and voluptuous characteristic of the Empire or Regency style.

The beehive clock contains glass tablet decorations in frosted and cut designs. Later glass was treated by the process called decalcomania. Chauncey Jerome preferred to substitute a small looking glass for the decorated tablet. He was also among the first to produce inexpensive one-day brass movements in the beehive case clock.

20-0 Beehive Clock (color plate)
"Round Gothic"
Jonathan Clark Brown
Forestville Manufacturing Company
Bristol, CT, c. 1850
H. 18½ ", W. 10 ", D. 3¾ ", Dial 7 "

Victorian period, Empire influence, rosewood and veneer case with heavy moldings, rosewood bezel; 8-day spring equalized power fusee brass movement; white painted metal dial, raised chapter ring, Roman chapters, spade hands, time and strike. On dial "J. C. Brown, Bristol, Ct. U.S." On label "Eight Day Brass Clocks . . . Forestville Manufacturing Comp'y/J. C. Brown, Bristol, Conn." **(E)**

NAWCCM, Inc.

20-1 Beehive Clock
William Thompson
Baltimore, MD, c. 1790-1800

Federal period, Gothic influence, mahogany case, brass bezel and feet, brass screens at sides; white painted dial, Roman chapters, time and strike. Earliest known American beehive case. On dial "Will.ᵐ Thompson/Baltimore." **(D)**

H. and R. Sandor, Inc.

20-2 Beehive Clock
Terry and Andrews
Bristol, CT, c. 1847
H. 19¾", W. 10¾"

Victorian period, Empire influence, gilded gesso design case, metal bezel, glass tablet etched with heart design; 8-day brass lyre-shaped movement; white painted zinc dial, Roman chapters, separate brass alarm ring in center, time, strike and alarm. **(E)**

20-3 Beehive Timepiece
Waterbury Clock Co.
Waterbury, CT, c. 1870
H. 8", W. 5"

Victorian period, Gothic influence, wood case with penny feet, diamond-shaped two-toned inlaid design, inlaid band follows beehive form; white painted dial, Arabic chapters, separate second hand and dial, time only. **(F)**

B.C. & R. Roan, Inc.

20-4 Beehive Timepiece
Ansonia Clock Company
Ansonia, CT, c. 1880
H. 10"

Victorian period, Gothic influence, mahogany veneer case, wood bezel, floral design on tablet; 8-day spring movement; white painted dial, Roman chapters, time only. (Photographed with a French carriage timepiece.) **(F)**

Robert W. Skinner, Inc.

20-5 Beehive Clock
Seth Thomas Clock Company
Thomaston, CT, c. 1890
H. 11", W. 6½", D. 4½"

Victorian period, Gothic influence, mahogany case, stylized butterfly inlay, brass bezel and bun feet; white painted dial, slow-fast mechanism, Arabic chapters, time and strike. On dial "Made by Seth Thomas in U.S.A." On movement "Made by/S.T./U.S.A." **(F)**

Deborah Batdorf

20-6 Beehive Clock
Seth Thomas Clock Company
Thomaston, CT, c. 1890
H. 11½", W. 7½", Dial 4¾"

Victorian period, Gothic and Federal influences, wood case, brass penny feet, brass bezel; 8-day movement; white dial, Arabic chapters, time and strike. On dial "Made in U.S.A." **(F)**

20-7 Beehive Clock
"Sonora Chimes"
Seth Thomas Clock Company
Thomaston, CT, c. 1930
H. 14¾", W. 10", D. 7¼"

Modern period, mahogany beehive case, brass bezel; 8-day spring-driven movement with Whittington and Westminster chimes; silvered dial, Arabic chapters, fast-slow mechanism, time, strike, and alarm. On dial "Seth Thomas/Sonora Chime/Made by Seth Thomas in USA." **(F)**

NAWCCM, Inc.

21 | Box or Cottage Clocks

Eli Terry's famous 1816 patent covering "a new and useful improvement on the thirty-hour brass and wooden clocks" with, in all likelihood, the unusual "off center" pendulum on a strap frame movement, was first housed in an experimental or box-style case later called a cottage clock. Terry's first contract for 4000 wooden wagon-on-the-walls and his 1816 patent which led eventually to the pillar and scroll models put the Connecticut towns of Bristol, Plymouth, and Farmington in the forefront of the clock manufacturing world. It appears that Seth Thomas, a joiner hired by Terry in 1808, was the actual producer of the first box clocks—that is, he cased and sold the first wooden four-wheeled train box clocks between 1816 and 1818. In 1818 Thomas was licensed by Terry to make the movements in any quantity. He was sold the "shop rights" so long as he was willing to pay a royalty to Terry of fifty cents for each movement made. In 1822 Thomas was given the rights without charge. So although the credit for the experimental box clock belongs to Terry, it was Thomas who made and produced most of the first American wooden-movement clocks which were available to both the mechanic class and the merchant. Later box clocks, commonly referred to as cottage clocks, were neither horologically, technologically, nor historically significant.

The collector will generally be able to distinguish between early box clocks and later cottage clocks: cottage clocks are smaller, less expensive clocks usually identified by their decorated doors and uncomplicated movements. The term "box clock" is preferably reserved for the Terry and Thomas experimental models and for the larger thin-framed clocks.

21-O Cottage Clock (color plate)
Waterbury Clock Company
Waterbury, CT, c. 1857
H. 13¼ ", W. 9½ ", D. 4½ "

Victorian period, Empire influence, molded rosewood deep case, gold, red, and black winged owl painted and gilded on lower glass panel; 8-day movement, spring-driven brass movement; white painted tin dial, Roman chapters, time and strike. On label "Waterbury Clock Co.,/Waterbury, Conn./Manufacturers of Eight Day and Thirty Hour/Brass Clocks and Timepieces." **(F)**

Irvin G. Schorsch III

21-1 Box Clock
Eli Terry, Inventor
Cased, sold, and probably made
    by Seth Thomas
Plymouth, CT, c. 1815-18
H. 20", W. 14", D. 4⁷⁄₁₆"

Empire period, wooden dove-tailed case, veneer on door, single glass panel with Arabic chapters painted on door; lead weights hang on either side of pendulum; count wheel movement mounted on back, 8-day time and strike. Eli Terry patented the movement June 12, 1816. In October, 1818 Terry sold the "shop rights" to Seth Thomas. **(D)**

The National Museum of History and Technology, Smithsonian Institution

21-2 Cottage Clock
J. C. Brown, Forestville Manufacturing Company
Bristol, CT, c. 1836
H. 14³⁄₄"

Empire period, wood veneer case on deep base, mirror in door; 30-hour spring brass movement; white painted metal dial, black and gilt design painted in four spandrel corners, Roman chapters, time and strike. **(F)**

21-3 Cottage Clock
Smith & Goodrich
Bristol, CT, c. 1847
H. 15½"

Victorian period, Empire influence, rosewood veneer molded frame case, floral design painted on lower glass door; 30-hour spring movement with fuses; white painted metal dial, Roman chapters, time and strike. **(F)**

21-4 Cottage Clock
"Cottage Extra"
Jerome & Company
New Haven, CT, c. 1850
H. 13", W. 9¾", D. 4½"

Victorian period, rosewood veneer case; design in red, turquoise, and gilt on lower glass; 8-day brass spring movement; white painted tin dial, blue painted flowers in spandrel corners, raised chapter ring, Roman chapters, moon-shaped hands, time and strike. On label "Cottage Extra Eight-Day Striking/ . . . Jerome & Co./New Haven, Conn., U.S.A." **(F)**

The Main Street Press

21-5 Cottage Clock
"No. 2 Model"
Jerome & Company
New Haven, CT, c. 1850
H. 11¾", W. 7¾", D. 3½"

Victorian period, pine case, painted wheat and medallion designs on glass tablet; 30-hour brass spring movement with alarm; white painted metal dial, blue flowers in spandrel corners, brass alarm ring, time, strike and alarm. On label "Jerome & Co., New Haven, Conn." **(F)**

NAWCCM, Inc.

21-6 Cottage Clock
"Cottage Extra"
Ansonia Brass & Copper Co.
Ansonia, CT, c. 1854
H. 12", W. 3¾", D. 3¾"

Victorian period, pine case with veneer on door, painted flowers on lower glass tablet; 30-hour brass spring movement with alarm; white painted tin dial, Roman chapters, brass alarm ring, blue arabesques in spandrel corners, time, strike, and alarm. On label "30-Hour Time/Cottage Extra/Ansonia Brass & Copper Co." **(F)**

The Main Street Press

21-7 Box Clock
"Crane's Torsion Pendulum Clock"
The Year Clock Company, manufacturer
Aaron D. Crane, inventor of movement
New York, NY, c. 1855
H. 20¼", W. 11¼", D. 5¼"

Victorian period, walnut and veneer case, etched glass tablet; 8-day torsion pendulum (i.e., bob swings in horizontal plane at right angles to the line of the metal ribbon suspension; used where long vibrations of a slow rate are required as in a 400-day clock); white painted wood dial, flower in spandrel corners, Roman chapters, time and strike. On top of dial "J.R. Mills & Co., New York." On bottom of dial "A.D. Crane's Patent." On label "Crane's Patent Eight Day Clocks manufactured by/The Year Clock Company . . . New York." [J.R. Mills & Co. became The Year Clock Company.] **(E)**

NAWCCM, Inc.

21-8 Cottage Timepiece
Waterbury Clock Company
Waterbury, CT, c. 1858
H. 12", W. 8", D. 3½"

Victorian period, painted green wood and glass tablet with Greek geometric design; 30-hour brass spring movement with alarm; white painted dial, Roman chapters, brass alarm ring, green scrolls in spandrel corners, time and alarm. **(F)**

NAWCCM, Inc.

21-9 Cottage Clock
Maker unknown
Place unknown, c. 1860
H. 12", W. 8¾", D. 4"

Victorian period, rosewood veneer case, green and gilt on glass tablet; 30-hour spring movement; white painted dial, Roman chapters, moon-shaped hands, green scrolls in spandrel corners, time and strike. **(F)**

NAWCCM, Inc.

21-10 Cottage Clock
Ansonia Clock Company
Ansonia, CT, c. 1865
H. 13½", W. 10½", D. 4¼"

Victorian period, rosewood veneer, molded case, gold band around door, looking glass tablet; 30-hour brass spring movement; white painted metal dial, Roman chapters, brass alarm ring, flowers in spandrel corners, time, strike, and alarm. On label "Ansonia Clock Co., Ansonia, Conn." **(F)**

NAWCCM, Inc.

21-11 Cottage Clock
Seth Thomas Clock Company
Thomaston, CT, c. 1870
H. 14½", W. 10", D. 4¼"

Victorian period, flowers painted on lower glass tablet; 8-day brass spring-driven movement; white painted, tin dial, Roman chapters, time and strike. On dial "Made in U.S.A." On label "Seth Thomas/Thomaston, Conn./Warranted Good." **(F)**

Private Collection

22 | Pillar and Scroll Clocks

Between the years 1818 and 1822, Eli Terry invented a pillar and scroll shelf case, probably inspired by the typical Federal-period grandfather clock characterized by its thin, scrolled, arched pediment, its splayed or tapered feet, and its columnar supports. (**Pillars** are detached round or square supporting structures, as distinct from **pilasters** which are rectangular, merely decorative, and engaged or attached to the case. **Columns** are round pillars.) The 1821 Terry case housed an improved box clock movement attached to a wooden dial with a five-wheeled train, a center-mounted outside escapement (or, more rarely, an inside-outside escapement), and an escape wheel with forty-two teeth. The scrolled clock improvements were, in KennethtRoberts expert opinion, mainly economical refinements.

Following Terry in the production of this first popularly-priced wooden model were Samuel Terry, one of Eli's younger brothers; Seth Thomas, who put Terry's off-center box movement into a pillar and scroll case; and Ephraim Downs, Chauncey Jerome, and Silas Hoadley, all trained in the woodworking trades. Although Heman Clark also made pillar and scrolls before 1824, his movements were designed in cast-brass and cut-steel pinions instead of the original wood type. Of the six wooden-works clockmakers, Ephraim Downs and Samuel Terry produced the movements for other merchants who applied their own labels and cases. Consequently, the wooden-works pillar and scroll package has been identified with at least thirty-five different clockmakers before 1834. Clocks with wooden works were successful until 1840 when cast brass became available in America and sheet brass became a viable commodity.

One of Eli and Samuel Terry's stylistic variations of the pillar and scroll case was called the "whale's tail." It was a carved fretwork like that found on grandfather clock cases from rural areas of Maine, and it obviously suggested the outline of a whale's tail. A movement variation of the Terry patent was created by Norris North in 1822 and was called the "Torrington" or "horizontal movement." It rested across the inside top of the case instead of being positioned in the usual vertical direction. In another case variation used by Chauncey Jerome and Orrin Hart, the pillars were replaced with a set of reeded pilasters. Even a "groaner"—or noisy, overhead striking movement—did not detract from the popularity of the pillar and scroll case type.

22-O Pillar and Scroll Clock (color plate)
Eli Terry, inventor
Made and sold by E. Terry & Sons
Plymouth, CT, c. 1823
H. 31 ", W. 15 ", D. 3¼ "

Empire period, Hepplewhite influence, walnut veneer case with brass urn finials, free-standing columns, French tapered feet, two large buildings and landscape scene painted on lower glass tablet, oval for viewing pendulum in center; 30-hour weight-driven wood movement; white painted wood dial with flowers in spandrel corners, Arabic chapters, time and strike. On label "Patent Clocks invented by Eli Terry. Made and sold at Plymouth Connecticut by E. Terry & Sons." **(D)**

Private Collection

22-1 Pillar and Scroll Clock
Seth Thomas
Plymouth, CT, c. 1818
H. 28 ″, W. 17½ ″, D. 4¼ ″

Empire period, Hepplewhite influence, mahogany veneer case with urn-shaped brass finials, top of door frame stamped with Roman numeral "V", glass door once painted with landscape scene; visible 2″ escape wheel, off-center pendulum, 8-day strap movement of cherry and oak; back plate stamped "5"; white painted wood dial, landscape and buldings painted on dial, leaves painted in spandrel corners, Arabic chapters, time and strike. Only known example of second of five pre-production styles leading to standard model of Seth Thomas shelf clocks. **(D)**

The National Museum of History and Technology, Smithsonian Institution

22-2 Pillar and Scroll Clock
Eli Terry
Plymouth, CT, c. 1818
H. 29½ ″, W. 17⅞ ″, D. 4¼ ″

Empire period, Hepplewhite influence, mahogany veneer case, scrolled pediment, brass urn finials, baseboard with narrow molded edge; though glass door panel appears as two pieces like later clocks with wood between tablet and dial glass, it is only one panel with painted imitation-wood separation; landscape and pendulum bob oval painted in lower section; outside escapement with pendulum hanging down in front of dial, oak front and back movement plates, lead weights; white painted dial with flowers in spandrel corners, Arabic chapters, time and strike. Label reads "Patent, Made and sold by Eli Terry, Plymouth, Conn." Sun calendar (January through June at left and July through December at right) border the inside label. **(D)**

The National Museum of History and Technology, Smithsonian Institution

22-3 Pillar and Scroll Clock
Seth Thomas
Plymouth, CT, c. 1818
H. 29½", W. 17⅝", D. 4⅜"

Empire period, Hepplewhite influence, wood veneer case with scrolled pediment and brass urn-shaped finials; inside-outside escapement, off-center pendulum, landscape and two buildings painted on lower glass panel; white painted dial, Arabic chapters, time and strike. On label "Patent Clock/Made and Sold by/Seth Thomas;/and Warranted if Well Used." **(D)**

W.G. Harding

22-4 Pillar and Scroll Clock
"No. 5"
Eli Terry
Plymouth, CT, c. 1818
H. 30½", W. 17½", D. 4¾"
Empire period, Hepplewhite influence, mahogany and veneer case, scrolled pediment, brass urn finials, seascape scene and floral and oak leaf border painted in lower glass panel; white painted dial with gilt scrolls in spandrel corners, Roman chapters, time and strike. On label "Patent Clocks/Made and Sold at Plymouth, Conn./Eli Terry/Inventor and Patentee . . . N.B. The public may be assured that this kind of clock will run as long without repairs, and be as durable and accurate for keeping time, as any kind of common clock whatever." **(D)**

Mr. and Mrs. Joseph H. Reese. Jr.

22-5 Pillar and Scroll Timepiece
Joseph Ives
Bristol, CT, c. 1820
H. 27", W. 14"
Empire period, Hepplewhite influence, mahogany veneer case and tiger maple pillars, three brass urn-shaped finials, shaped apron and tapered feet, buildings painted on glass tablet; 8-day weight-driven brass movement; white painted iron dial with flowers painted in spandrel corners and gilt design around dial, Roman chapters, time (strikes once on the hour). **(D)**

22-6 Pillar and Scroll Clock
Eli Terry
Plymouth, CT, c. 1820-30
H. 31¼", W. 17½", D. 4½"

Empire period, Hepplewhite influence, mahogany and veneer case with brass urn finials, masonic iconography painted on lower glass tablet, clear oval glass to see pendulum bob; 8-day movement; white painted dial, flowers painted in spandrel corners, Arabic chapters, time and strike. On label "Patent Clocks, made and sold at Plymouth, Connecticut, by Eli Terry, Inventor and Patentee." **(D)**

Israel Sack, Inc., N.Y.C.

22-7 Pillar and Scroll Clock
"Perfected Wood Clock"
  (maker's title)
Eli Terry
Plymouth, CT, c. 1822
H. 31", W. 17", D. 4½"

Empire period, Hepplewhite influence, mahogany veneer case with scrolled pediment and brass urn finials; 8-day movement; landscape painted on lower glass tablet; white painted dial, gilt chain painted inside chapter ring, roses painted in spandrel corners, Arabic chapters, time and strike. **(D)**

The National Museum of History and Technology, Smithsonian Institution

22-8 Pillar and Scroll Clock
Eli Terry & Son
Plymouth, CT, c. 1825
H. 31¼"

Empire period, Hepplewhite influence, walnut veneer case, shaped apron, tapered feet, three brass urn-shaped finials, allegorical landscape mourning scene painted on glass tablet; 30-hour wooden movement; white painted dial with gilt scrolls in spandrel corners and flower basket painted above numeral 6, Arabic chapters, time and strike. **(D)**

22-9 Pillar and Scroll Clock
Erastus Hodges
Torrington, CT, c. 1831
H. 27½ ", W. 13¼ "

Empire period, Hepplewhite influence, mahogany veneer case, scrolled top, three brass urn-shaped finials, shaped apron, tapered feet, landscape and house painted on glass tablet; flower border painted above and below landscape, painted oval pendulum bob; white painted dial with flowers painted in spandrel corners, Arabic chapters, time and strike. **(D)**

22-10 Pillar and Scroll Clock
Jacob D. Custer
Norristown, PA, c. 1840
H. 38 "

Victorian period, Hepplewhite and Empire influences, mahogany and veneer case, elongated swan's neck scrolls ending in carved sunflowers, wood urn finials, double button feet; 8-day brass movement, unusual hammer arrangement; white painted dial, flower basket painted in arch over dial, snail shells painted in spandrel corners, Arabic chapters, separate second hand and dial, time and strike. On dial "J.D. Custer/Norristown/Patent." **(D)**

Greenfield Village and Henry Ford Museum

22-11 Pillar and Scroll Timepiece (Variation)
John Taber
Saco, ME, c. 1815

Empire period, Federal influence, mahogany veneer and maple case with swan's neck scrolls in broken arch, wooden finials, wooden ball feet, reeded pilasters, center panel in wood, lower panel with grand house, lake, boat, and trees painted on glass, pendulum bob oval in center of lower panel; brass-bushed, iron-plated, 8-day movement; white painted dial, green leaves painted in spandrel corners, Roman chapters, time only. On dial "John Taber." **(D)** Compare with looking-glass timepiece (section 10).

Robert W. Skinner, Inc.

23 | Lighthouse Timepieces

The lighthouse timepiece—a patented alarm made by the Willard family and presumably named after the Eddystone Lighthouse in Plymouth, England—is characterized by its handsome high-style case. The lighthouse movement is generally an eight-day mechanism housed in cases made of rosewood or mahogany. A so-called "bridal" or "marriage" lighthouse timepiece painted white and gilded like the banjo presentation timepiece, was a specialty of Simon Willard.

Lighthouse cases rise up as shaped columns and end in a white enamel dial, with the movement behind it and with a horizontally-placed bell and a hand-blown glass cover. The feet generally take one of the two typical Empire forms—two front gilded balls or two front lion's paws. Both are true to Egyptian and Roman archetypes. Although beautiful in its time, the lighthouse timepiece did not succeed as a useful timekeeper. It has become a rarity today and, like the misstruck coin, is now a clock collector's dream.

23-0 Lighthouse Timepiece (color plate)
"Eddystone Lighthouse" or "Bridal Timepiece"
Simon Willard
Roxbury, MA, c. 1820-30
H. 30″, W. 9½″, D. 9½″

Empire period, classical influence, painted white case with gilt and blue decoration; classical building painted on wooden base; gilt ball feet, glass dome and finial; brass movement, alarm wheel and bell; white painted dial, Roman chapters, time and alarm. "Simon Willard's Patent, Roxbury." **(A)**

Israel Sack, Inc., N.Y.C.

23-1 Lighthouse Timepiece
Simon Willard
Roxbury, MA, c. 1820
H. 30", W. 9", D. 9"

Empire period, classical influence, mahogany case with octagonal base, a tapered, circular upper case supporting movement and glass dome; 8-day movement; brass dial, bell on top of dial, Roman chapters, separate alarm ring, typical Willard arrow hands, time and alarm. On dial "Simon Willard/Roxbury." **(A)**

23-2 Lighthouse Timepiece
Simon Willard
Roxbury, MA, c. 1820-30
H. 30½"

Empire period, classical influence, columnar mahogany case on rectangular base, rococo brass feet, laurel wreath and cherub brass ornament on base, horizontal bell, blown glass dome with finial; white enameled dial, alarm ring in center; Roman chapters, moon-shaped hands, time and alarm, once-on-the-hour strike. **(A)**

H. & R. Sandor, Inc.

23-3 Lighthouse Timepiece
Simon Willard & Son
Roxbury, MA, c. 1822-30
H. 30", D. 8¼"

Empire period, classical influence, mahogany case with chased brass molding around top of base, top of wooden column, and dial; cylindrical base stands on typical Empire brass ball feet; brass cornucopia, shell, and fern motif decorate base; blown glass dome with finial covers dial and movement; horizontally placed bell with small chased-brass fire gilded finial; white enameled dial, Roman chapters, time and once-on-the-hour strike. On dial "Simon Willard & Son's/Patent." **(A)**

Israel Sack, Inc., N.Y.C.

23-4 Lighthouse Timepiece
Simon Willard
Boston, MA, c. 1824-25
H. 29½", Diam. 9¼"

Empire period, classical influence, mahogany and mahogany-veneer case, pine secondary wood, brass, glass, and sulphur; sulphide bust of Marquis de Lafayette on base imposed on radiating fan, brass ball feet; bell above dial rests horizontally instead of vertically; glass dome and glass finial; white enameled dial, Roman chapters, time and once-on-the-hour strike. On dial "Simon Willard & Sons/Patent." **(A)**

The White House

23-5 Lighthouse Timepiece
Simon Willard
Roxbury, MA, c. 1825
H. 26½"

Empire period, classical influence, columnar mahogany case on octagonal base, chased brass molding around top of base, top of column, and around dial; brass cornucopia, shell, and ferns rest on top of bell, blown-glass dome with finial covers dial and movement, white, enameled dial, moon-shaped hands, Roman chapters, time and once-on-the-hour strike. **(A)**

Sotheby Parke Bernet

23-6 Lighthouse Timepiece
Simon Willard & Son
Roxbury, MA, c. 1825
H. 26½"

Empire period, classical influence, columnar wood case and octagonal base, molding around base, brass molding around top of base and top of case, glass dome, brass rope design around dial, brass ornament above dial; deadbeat escapement, half-second pendulum; white painted dial, Roman chapters, time only. **(A)**

24 | Column Clocks

The column clock, variously referred to as "gilt column," "side column," "late classical," "hollow column," and "cornice and column" clocks is simply a two-column case with a low or molded Empire base and an architectural but flat cornice top. It was made as early as 1825 and as late as 1885 in New York, Connecticut, and Massachusetts manufactories. Like pillar and scroll, stenciled splat, and carved splat clocks, the flat-cornice column clock reflects the styles of case furniture especially popular in the early 1850s.

Large "S"- and "C"-scroll forms, and large ogee boards replaced the small classical motifs which ornamented clock cases of the Federal period. Rodney Brace of Massachusetts; Clark, Gilbert, & Company, E. O. Goodwin, the New Haven Clock Company, and Seth Thomas, all of Connecticut; and William A. Bradshaw and Asa Munger of New York were among the manufacturers of column clocks. Chauncey Jerome offered an especially fine gilded variation which was probably meant to commemorate special occasions just as gilt on Willard banjo and lighthouse timekeepers signified important events.

One of the most intriguing of columnar types was the late Empire hollow column design (24-3). It is associated largely with Luman Watson, a famous Ohio clock manufacturer and also with George Marsh of Bristol, Connecticut. The large front columns do more than support the heavy architectural cornice. They allow the weights to drop invisibly and add a popular, bulky aesthetic to the case form.

Heman Clark, who developed the first mass-produced spring-driven brass-movement shelf clock in America, housed some of his movements in carved or smooth column cases with paw feet and flat cornices. They were designed for him by Alfred Platt of Waterbury, Connecticut, who also designed cases for the clock manufacturer Mark Leavenworth. Like most casemakers, Platt created his designs to suit the requirements of the movement as well as to suit the public taste. For Leavenworth he made larger cases than for Clark in order to provide room for the weights needed to power Leavenworth's wooden mechanism.

24-0 Column Clock (color plate)
"Gilt Column"
Seth Thomas Clock Company
Thomaston, CT, c. 1833
H. 32¼", W. 16¼", D. 4¼"

Victorian period, Empire influence, rosewood case, large engaged gilt columns, bold ogee plinths below columns, flat cornice, two women admiring jewelry painted on lower glass tablet; 8-day brass movement; white painted metal dial, raised chapter ring, Roman chapters, spade hands, time and strike. On dial "S T." On label "Seth Thomas/Thomaston, CT. . . . Case, Lockwood & Brainard, printers, Hartford." **(E)**

NAWCCM, Inc.

24-1 Column Clock
Norris North
Torrington, CT, c. 1823
H. 24¼", W. 13⅝"

Empire period, wood veneer case, bronzed and black painted columns, flat top, view of Quebec painted on lower glass tablet; 30-hour east-west wood movement; white painted dial, painted design in spandrel corners, Arabic chapters, diamond-shaped hands, time and strike. **(E)**

24-2 Column Clock
Curtis & Clark
Plymouth, CT, c. 1825
H. 22¾", W. 12½", D. 4¼"

Empire period, Egyptian influence, miniature mahogany case, ring and leaf carved and engaged columns, paw feet, house and landscape painted on lower panel of glass door; 7-day brass movement, rack and snail strike, Swiss springs in barrels; white painted iron dial, flowers painted on spandrel corners, separate second hand and dial, Arabic chapters, time and strike. On label "Eight Day Brass Clocks Made by Curtis & Clark. Plymouth, Con." **(E)**

W. G. Harding

24-3 Column Clock
"Hollow Column"
Asa Munger
Auburn, NY, c. 1830
H. 40", W. 18¼"

Empire period, mahogany case, carved top, finials, rosettes, and Corinthian capitals, sheet-iron columns, painted with black and gilt, mirror door, weights drop inside hollow columns, brass bezel; white painted dial with gold numeral bands, Roman chapters, time and strike. Although this case resembles Column and Carved Splat cases, it has been listed as a Column Clock because its most important feature is its pair of hollow columns. **(E)**

American Clock & Watch Museum

24-4 Column Clock
George Marsh & Company
Bristol, CT, c. 1832
H. 37½", W. 17½"

Empire period, walnut veneer case with round hollow columns for weights resting on deep base with ball feet, fruit basket painted on glass tablet; 8-day weight-driven brass strap movement; white painted dial, Arabic chapters, time and strike. **(E)**

24-5 Column Clock
William Beach
Hartford, CT, c. 1834

Empire period, mahogany case, acanthus leaf and ring-carved engaged columns, flat cornice, unusual floral-carved feet resembling volutes; seascape and gilt leaf border painted on lower glass tablet; white painted dial with scrolls in spandrel corners, Roman chapters, time and strike. **(E)**

Robert W. Skinner, Inc.

24-6 Column Clock
Birge, Mallory & Company
Bristol, CT, c. 1840
H. 37", W. 17½", D. 5½"

Victorian period, classical influence, mahogany and veneer, pine case, flat cornice, freestanding columns, Empire ogee molding below columns, two ball front feet, two back feet turned; house and landscape scene painted on middle and lower glass tablets, painted diamond-shaped pendulum bob; 8-day brass movement; white painted dial, time and strike. Movement stamped ''BM&CO.'' Label printed by Lathrop of Hartford. **(E)**

Compare with Double Decker clocks (25-2).

NAWCCM, Inc.

24-7 Column Clock
M. Welton
New York, NY, c. 1840
H. 28½", W. 19½", D. 6"

Victorian period, classical influence, mahogany and veneer case with shortened half-round heavy 3" diameter engaged columns, heavy base, painting of Girard College on lower panel of main glass door, lowest glass door panel has stylized painted flower; weight-driven; white painted dial, Roman chapters, time and strike. On glass "Girard College." **(E)**

The National Museum of History and Technology, Smithsonian Institution

24-8 Column Clock
Sperry & Shaw
New York, NY, c. 1848
H. 27"

Victorian period, classical influence, walnut case, ogee molded board and flat cornice above dial, free standing columns, ogee molded base, landscape scene painted in lower panel; white painted dial with flowers in spandrel corners, Roman chapters, time and strike. **(E)**

B. C. & R. Roan, Inc.

24-9 Column Clock
Franklin C. Andrews
New York, NY, and Bristol, CT, c. 1843
H. 26½"

Victorian period, classical influence, walnut case, flat cornice, free standing columns, wide Empire base, European landscape painted on lower panel; white painted dial, Roman chapters, alarm ring exposed, time and strike. **(E)**

B. C & R. Roan, Inc.

24-10 Column Clock
Irenus Atkins, probably as part of the firm Atkins, Whiting & Company
Bristol, CT, c. 1850
H. 17⅝", W. 13½", D. 5¾"

Victorian period, Empire influence, rosewood case, upper glass door painted, lower door mirrored; 30-day wagon spring designed by Joseph Ives; white painted dial, Roman chapters, time and strike. **(E)**

W. G. Harding

24-11 Column Clock
Seth Thomas
Plymouth Hollow, CT, c. 1850-56
H. 26", W. 14¾", D. 4½"

Victorian period, classical influence, rosewood veneer case, engaged gilt columns, eagle, fruit, and leaf designs painted on glass tablet; brass movement; white painted tin dial, Roman chapters, flowers in spandrel corners, time and strike. On label "Brass Clocks/Made and Sold by/Seth Thomas,/Plymouth Hollow, Conn. . . ; [label printed by the] steam press of Elihu Geer, Hartford, Conn." **(E)**

NAWCCM, Inc.

24-12 Column Clock
Seth Thomas
Plymouth Hollow, CT, c. 1860
H. 26", W. 15½", D. 4¼"

Victorian period, classical influence, mahogany and veneer case, two sets of marbleized freestanding columns, gilded capitals and bases, Italian scene painted on glass tablet; 30-hour brass movement with "wafer" weights for power; white painted metal dial, raised chapter ring, blue flowers in spandrel corners, time and strike. On label "Seth Thomas/Plymouth Hollow, Conn." **(E)**

NAWCCM, Inc.

24-13 Column Clock
**"London Architectural" model
Irenus Atkins, probably a principal of the Atkins Clock Company
Bristol, CT, c. 1860
H. 16⅞", W. 13"**

Victorian period, rosewood case, engaged columns flat cornice, heavy architectural base; 30-day spring-driven fusee movement; white painted dial, Roman chapters, time and strike. In 1856, Joseph Ives wrote to Irenus Atkins to forbid further manufacture of Ives's wagon-spring clocks. Atkins consequently adapted his column clock to affect a 30-day spring-fusee movement.

W. C. Harding

24-14 Column Timepiece
**"Twin Glass Column"
Maker unknown
U.S.A., c 1880
H. 16", W. 9", D. 4½"**

Victorian period, metal and crystal case and columns, metal bezel; 30-hour movement; white painted dial, Arabic chapters, spade hands, time only. **(F)**

NAWCCM, Inc.

24-15 Column Clock
**"Gilt Column"
Seth Thomas Clock Company
Thomaston, CT, c. 1880
H. 32¼", W. 18¼", D. 5⅞"**

Victorian period, classical influence, rosewood case with gilt columns; flat cornice, geometric design on glass tablets; 8-day weight-driven movement; white painted dial, Roman chapters, time and strike. On front plate Seth Thomas trademark is stamped. Similar clocks listed earlier in 1864 catalogue. Label by Case, Lockwood & Brainard of Hartford. **(E)**

NAWCCM, Inc.

25 | Double and Triple Deckers

The first "double-decker" clock cases with separate upper and lower doors, separate locks and keys, as well as upper and lower free-standing smooth columns appeared early in the 1820s, housing high-grade brass eight-day movements. Heman Clark and Miles Morse, the latter having worked for a brief time with Clark, are associated with these early, delicate double-decker cases. The Clark and Morse cases were lighter and smaller than those of their contemporaries who were already working in the more stolid Empire style.

In 1830 Elias Ingraham, working for Chauncey and Lawson Ives, made what he called a "new fashioned" case, a boldly carved multi-tiered case with the new Empire paw feet. His muscular clocks were successful nationwide. Clockmakers assembled and/or peddled them in the South as well as in the North, lending great stylistic variety to tastemakers within the bounds of what was technologically possible. Customers could order their double or triple columns carved, fluted, or gilded. They could specify painted glass tablets or looking-glass doors, flat cornices, carved fretwork, or stencil-decorated splats. One Ingraham triple-decker boasted fluted pilasters on the base, two whole columns in the center, and half columns each side of the dial. One variation, though rare, is the ogee-molded double decker without two sets of tiered columns, but with double doors.

Customers could also order their tiered clocks with one of a variety of movements—wooden, short pendulums with cases made by Rollin and Irenus Atkins; brass-bushed thirty-hour wood movements by Chauncey and Nobel Jerome; full-brass movements by the Jeromes; or Birge, Mallory movements in Dyer, Wadsworth and Company cases. They could also ask for tiered clocks made by Spencer, Hotchkiss and Company, R. and J. B. Terry, as well as the first "decker" makers, Heman and Sylvester Clark. From 1824 to 1830 Lucius B. Bradley and James Bishop offered double deckers with brass movements made by Clark as well as with the Terry-type movements made of wood.

Movements and cases, then, were not always or often made by the same men. Where the name on the dial of an eighteenth-century clock usually refers to the man who made the movement, the name on the dial of a nineteenth- or twentieth-century clock usually refers to the assembler or retailer.

25-O Triple Decker Clock (color plate)
Birge, Peck & Company
Bristol, CT, c. 1849
H. 34", W. 15", D. 4"

Victorian period, classical influence, rosewood veneer case with three glass panels (two painted), triple sets of engaged columns (two sets marbleized, one set gilt), architectural volutes atop columns, carved gilt spread eagle spans cornice; 8-day brass movement with "rolling pinion steel pivots; white painted dial, Roman chapters, time and strike. On label is picture of a locomotive called "The Breeze," a pair of Corinthian columns, and "Brass Clocks Made and Sold by Birge, Peck & Co., Bristol, Conn." Label printed by "Press of Elihu Geer . . . Hartford." (Geer was the engraver of another fanciful steam locomotive, "Puffing Betsy.") **(E)**

Dr. and Mrs. George W. Scott, Jr.

25-1 Double Decker Clock
E. Terry & Sons
Plymouth, CT, c. 1825
H. 37½", W. 17¾", D. 5½"

Empire period, Roman and Egyptian influences, mahogany case, pineapple and acanthus leaf carving on engaged columns, spread eagle carved across top, house and landscape painted on lower glass panel; 8-day wood movement with mahogany plates; white painted dial, scrolls painted in spandrel corners, Roman chapters, separate second hand and dial, time and strike. On label "Goodwin & Co. . . Print . . . Hartford, Conn." **(E)**

W. G. Harding

25-2 Double Decker Clock
Eli Terry, Jr. & Co.
Terrysville, CT, c. 1830
H. 38½", W. 18½", D. 4½"

Empire period, Roman and Egyptian influences, mahogany and veneer case, indistinctly carved leaves and wheat on attached columns, spread eagle over acanthus leaf carving at top, paw feet, house and trees painted on lower door with clear oval in lower center; white painted dial with gilt scrolls in spandrel corners; 30-hour wood movement, Arabic chapters, time and strike. **(E)**

Greenfield Village and Henry Ford Museum

25-3 Triple Decker Clock
Riley Whiting; Orsamus Fyler,
   patentee
Winchester, CT, c. 1831
H. 40", W. 17½", D. 6½"

Empire period, mahogany and veneer case, glass and mirror panels; three sets of columns with pineapple, ring, and acanthus leaf carvings; carved pineapple finials, carved paw feet, carved flower basket on top; white painted dial with scrolls in spandrel corners, Roman chapters, time and strike. On label "Fyler's Patent . . . Riley Whiting." **(E)**

Index of American Design, National Gallery of Art, Washington

25-4 Triple Decker Clock
Spencer, Hotchkiss & Company
Salem Bridge (Naugatuck), CT, c. 1835
H. 31", W. 17", D. 5½"

Empire period, wood veneer case, three sets of columns (one set gilded), carved and gilded leaf and basket splat; 8-day brass weight-driven movement; white painted dial with designs in four spandrel corners, Roman chapters, time and strike. **(E)**

25-5 Triple Decker Clock
Barnes, Bartholemew Company
Bristol, CT, c. 1835
H. 36"

Empire period, Roman influence, wood veneer case, bronzed triple set of columns, carved and gilded leaf splat, "View near Natchez" painted on middle glass panel, wood lower panel; 30-hour weight-driven brass movement; white painted dial, flowers painted in center, gilt scrolls in spandrel corners, Roman chapters, time and strike. **(E)**

25-6 Triple Decker Clock
Dyer, Wadsworth & Company, manufacturer
Birge, Mallory & Company, probably movement maker
Augusta, GA; movement, CT, c. 1835
H. 40"

Empire period, classical influence, three sets of columns (one set gilded), two glass panels painted with designs, carved and gilded spread eagle on splat; 3-day weight-driven movement; white painted dial, Roman chapters, time and strike. Label printed by State Rights' Sentinel Office, Augusta. **(E)**

25-7 Triple Decker Clock
Cased and sold by Dyer, Wadsworth & Co.; movement probably made by Birge, Mallory & Co.
Augusta, GA and Bristol, CT, c. 1838
H. 40"

Empire period, Roman influence, painted wood and gilt case with triple columns, the upper and lower columns painted in black with base and capitals in gilt, the middle columns entirely of gilt, splat across top holds gilt spread wing eagle, circles on plinths at top resemble architectural details of the period; two of the three glass panels painted with flowers and leaf border, the lower panel with house, trees, and fence, a heart motif is centered in lower panel instead of usual pendulum bob oval; 8-day weight-driven movement; gilt scrolls painted in spandrel corners, black chapter ring, white Roman chapters, time and strike. On label "Patent Brass Eight Day Clocks." **(E)**

Greenfield Village and Henry Ford Museum

25-8 Double Decker Clock
"Miniature Double Decker," "10 & 2"
Forestville Manufacturing Company
Bristol, CT, c. 1842
H. 27½", W. 13¾", D. 5"

Victorian period, Empire influence, rosewood veneer case, double sets of engaged gilt split spindle columns, flat cornice, two houses and landscape painted on middle glass tablet, abstract design painted in black, blue, red and gilt on lower glass tablet; 8-day brass weight movement; white painted metal dial, Roman chapters, flowers in spandrel corners, raised chapter ring, time

and strike. On label "E. N. Welch,
J.C. Brown & C. Pomery. . . ."
Label printed by Joseph Hurlbut,
Hartford. **(E)**

26 | Column and Stenciled Splat Clocks

The most famous of the column and stenciled splat clock cases was made by Chauncey Jerome in 1827. Jerome himself wrote in his History of the American Clock Business that he had "invented a new case, somewhat larger then the Scroll top, which was called the Bronze Looking Glass." "This," he added, "was the richest looking and best clock that had ever been made for the price."

But Jerome did not invent the design of a "looking glass" below the dial plate. Joseph Ives had already incorporated it into his finely-made wall design of 1818 (see section 10). Jerome did, however, produce a cheaper **shelf** version with a long case, a stenciled design in bronze pigment on the top and side columns, and with the famous looking glass in the lower section of the door. Like the gilt- and ebony-stenciled chairs, beds, and mirrors in the early Empire high-style, Jerome's eagle-, flower-, and fruit-stencil motifs carried the decorative requirements of the domestic market into the domain of the horological tinkerer.

Although Chauncey Boardman made movements for Jerome in 1824, it was Nobel Jerome who designed the wooden thirty-hour "thin movement" controlled by a 17.4-inch pendulum for the first stenciled looking-glass clock. The case was about the size of a Terry pillar and scroll clock. By 1828 Jerome had modified the Terry five-train movement. He substituted an escape wheel with thirty-two teeth for the one with forty-two teeth and increased the pendulum to 15.4 inches.

Jeromes and Darrow manufactured their now scarce stenciled case with an eight-day wooden movement. Horologist Edward La Find has found three Pennsylvania-made brass eight-day movements housed in cases labeled "Jeromes and Darrow", a discovery which suggests the possibility that nineteenth-century shelf clocks as far away as Pennsylvania and Connecticut exchanged movements for dials, cases, and weights. George Mitchell, for example, put out a stenciled case with Boardman movements. Marsh, Gilbert & Company and Ephraim Downs sold stenciled looking-glass shelf clocks in Farmington until 1830. Thomas Barnes, Jr., and Elisha Welch traded bronzed stenciled-splat looking-glass shelf clocks in Bristol in 1831. Short-pendulum stenciled clock cases, probably made by Elias Ingraham and used by George Mitchell with Samuel Terry movements and "faces," were sold in 1830. The collector should note that clock labels sometimes document both the manufacturer of the movement and the assembler—e.g., "IMPROVED CLOCKS/Manufactured/by/SAMUEL TERRY/for/GEORGE MITCHELL/Bristol, Conn." By 1833, at least sixty-two makers had produced stenciled splat clocks with wooden movements.

26-O Column and Stenciled Splat Clock (color plate)
Eli Terry, inventor
Made and sold by E. Terry & Sons
Plymouth, CT, c. 1830
H. 29 ", W. 17 ", D. 4½ "

Empire period, Hepplewhite influence, walnut veneer case with bronze stenciled flowers and leaves on columns (ending in gilt capitals) bronze stencil of a fruit basket and cornucopias on splat, lion's paw feet; house, river, and trees painted on lower glass panel, oval to view pendulum in center; 30-hour wood movement; white painted dial with gold leaf circle in center, Arabic chapters, time and strike. On label "Patented Clocks, invented by Eli Terry. Made and sold at Plymouth, Connecticut, by E. Terry & Sons. Warranted if well used. Goodwin & Co. printers, Hartford, Conn." **(E)**

Irvin G. Schorsch III

26-1 Column and Stenciled Splat Clock
Eli Terry
Plymouth, CT, c. 1822
H. 26½ ", W. 16½ ", D. 4½ "

Empire period, Roman and Egyptian influences, mahogany veneer, painted stenciled case and columns, Doric capitals on columns, basket of fruit and fruit surround stenciled and painted, scene and pendulum bob oval painted on lower glass panel, carved paw feet; white painted dial, Arabic chapters, time and strike. **(E)**

Index of American Design, National Gallery of Art, Washington

26-2 Column and Stenciled Splat Clock
"Short Pendulum"
Eli Terry
Plymouth, CT, c. 1822
H. 28½", W. 15¾", D. 4"

Empire period, Egyptian influence, mahogany case with bronze stenciling on quarter round columns, carved paw feet, curved stenciled splat, houses painted in lower glass panel; wooden works, cast-iron weights; white painted dial with gilt scrolls in spandrel corners and gilt floral wreath in center, moon-type hands, Arabic chapters, time and strike. **(E)**

The National Museum of History and Technology, Smithsonian Institution

26-3 Column and Stenciled Splat Clock
Frederick Heiseley movement, probably a Connecticut case by Jeromes & Darrow
Harrisburg, PA; Bristol, CT, c, 1828
H. 38¾", W. 19", D. 5½"

Empire period, Duncan Phyfe influence, walnut and walnut veneer on pine, paint and gilt stenciled case, half round columns, stylized cornucopias with fruit painted on splat, mirror door, painted tray of fruit on lower panel of door; white painted dial, flowers painted in spandrel corners, diamond shapes painted in center with hand designs to match, Roman chapters, time and strike. Label on back reads "Superior/Brass Eight Day/Clocks,/ Manufactured expressly for Cyrus Eaton,/by/Frederick Heisely, sen./ Harrisburg, Pa./Warranted by/ Cyrus Eaton/and none sold except by his Agents." **(E)**

Pennsylvania Historical and Museum Commission, William Penn Memorial Museum

26-4 Column and Stenciled Splat Clock
E. & G. Bartholomew
Bristol, CT, c. 1828
H. 29 ", W. 17½ "

Empire period, Roman influence, wood veneer case, stenciled fruit basket on splat, bronzed columns, carved pineapple finials and paw feet, landscape painted on lower glass tablet; 30-hour weight-driven wood movement; white painted dial, Roman chapters, diamond-shaped hands, time and strike. **(E)**

26-5 Column and Stenciled Splat Timepiece
"Alarm Timepiece"
Silas Hoadley
Plymouth, CT, c. 1830
H. 25½ ", W. 13 ", D. 4 "

Empire period, Roman and Egyptian influences, mahogany and veneer case with bronze stenciled and black painted columns; basket of fruit and flowers designed on splat, carved paw feet with leaves carved above; house, mill, wheel, and stream painted on lower glass panel; "upside-down" wood movement; white painted dial with decoration in spandrel corners, Arabic chapters, second hand, time and alarm. **(E)**

Shelburne Museum, Inc.

26-6 Column and Stenciled Splat Clock
"Transition Looking Glass"
Riley T. Wood
Decatur, NY, c. 1830
H. 30 ", W. 18 ", D. 4 "

Empire period, walnut veneer case, black and bronzed engaged columns, stenciled splat, looking glass in lower door; 30-hour wood movement with escape wheel teeth cut on the radius; white painted wood dial, gilt scrolls in spandrel corners, Roman chapters, diamond-shaped hands, time and strike. **(E)**

NAWCCM, Inc.

26-7 Column and Stenciled Splat Clock
Silas Hoadley
Plymouth, CT, c. 1830
H. 37¼ ", W. 17 ", Dial 4¾ "

Empire period, wood veneer case, bronze stenciled columns and eagle splat, carved paw feet, mirror in lower door section, small bottom tablet has painted scene and weight-driven "Time Is Money"; 30-hour wood weight-driven "upside down" long pendulum movement; white painted dial, separate second hand, Arabic chapters, time and strike. **(E)**

26-8 Column and Stenciled Splat Clock
"Short Pendulum"
Eli Terry & Son
Plymouth, CT, c. 1830
H. 32¾", W. 17½", D. 4¼"

Empire period, walnut veneer case with black painted and gilded or bronzed engaged columns, gilded splat with eagle, cannons, and swords, looking glass on lower panel; 30-hour wood movement, short pendulum, weight-driven; white painted, wood dial, gilt scrolls in spandrel corners, gilt circle in center, diamond shaped bands, Arabic chapters, time and strike. Label printed by Joseph Hurlbut of Hartford. **(E)**

NAWCCM, Inc.

26-9 Column and Stenciled Splat Clock
Silas Hoadley, inventor
L. Smith, manufacturer
Plymouth and Bristol, CT, c. 1833
H. 24"

Empire period, wood veneer case, stenciled and painted columns and eagle splat, mirror in lower section of door; Hoadley alarm components with weight-driven pendulum movement; white painted dial with flowers painted in spandrel corners, separate second hand, Arabic chapters, time and strike. **(E)**

26-10 Column and Stenciled Splat Clock
George Marsh & Company
Farmington, CT, c. 1835
H. 33¼", W. 17¾"

Empire period, mahogany and veneer case with shaped fretwork stenciled with scrolled vines, engaged stenciled leaf columns; weight-driven pendulum movement; white painted dial with leaves painted in four spandrel corners with fruit in lower center of dial, Roman chapters, time and strike. **(E)**

27 | Column and Carved Splat Clocks

According to Milo Norton, a Bristol, Connecticut, historian writing in 1872, the creation of the column and carved splat clock case was a direct result of the competitive pursuits of George Mitchell, who wanted to find a novel clock case that would overwhelm both Terry's pillar and scroll and Jerome's "bronze looking glass" or stenciled clocks. In 1828 Mitchell hired the cabinetmaker Elias Ingraham to design a competitive case, and within the year Ingraham created his new carved Empire design. Turning Roman pineapple and acanthus leaf patterns into engaged columns, he placed bold lion's-paw feet at the base and designed carved patriotic eagle "fretwork heads" to complete the top. The result was the column and carved splat clock, known in its own day as a "patent mantle clock."

In addition to James Mitchell, Jeromes and Darrow and George Marsh, among others in the 1830s, worked with the column and carved splat form, each contributing a short-pendulum model. Like Marsh, some manufacturers used the looking glass in combination with carved splats to replace painted glass panels. E. Terry and Sons designed a transitional model best described as a composite of some pillar and scroll characteristics and some attributes of the carved-splat clock. Carved splats (and stenciled splats, as well) were so popular that clock historian Kenneth Roberts concluded that they put the makers of the original pillar and scroll clock out of business. At least twenty-nine clockmakers produced pillar and carved splat clocks with wooden movements by 1833.

27-O Column and Carved Splat Clock (color plate)
Henry Terry
Plymouth, CT, c. 1830
H. 32 ", W. 17½ ", D. 4¼ "

Empire period, Chippendale influence, wood veneer case, engaged acanthus-leaf and flower-carved columns, carved basket, flower and leaf splat, looking glass on door; 30-hour weight-driven movement; white painted wooden dial, gilt scrolls in spandrel corners, time and strike. On label "Invented by/Eli Terry/Made and Sold/at/Plymouth, Connecticut/by Henry Terry . . . Joseph Hurlbut, Printer, Hartford, Conn." **(E)**

NAWCCM, Inc.

27-1 Column and Carved Splat Clock
Eli Terry, designer
Marc Leavenworth, maker
Waterbury, CT, c. 1825
H. 23 ", W. 16 ", D. 4¼ "

Empire period, Roman and Egyptian influences, mahogany and veneer case, half-round columns carved in leaf and ring design with flower at top below capital, flowers and scrolls carved in top splat, front feet carved as lion's paws, landscape with house and floral design border painted in lower glass tablet; weight-driven movement; white painted dial with gilt chapter bands and gilt scrolls in spandrel corners, Arabic chapters, time and strike. **(E)**

Index of American Design, National Gallery of Art, Washington

27-2 Column and Carved Splat Clock
Jerome, Darrow and Company
Bristol, CT, c. 1825
H. 35¼ ", W. 18 "

Empire period, Roman influence, wood veneer case, carved spread eagle splat, half-round carved columns, two house and landscape scenes with black and gilt oak-leaf borders painted on lower glass tablet; 30-hour weight-driven wood movement; white painted wood dial with flowers painted in spandrel corners and in center of dial, Arabic chapters, diamond-shaped hands, time and strike. **(E)**

27-3 Column and Carved Splat Clock
Riley Whiting
Winchester, CT, c. 1828
H. 34 ", W. 16½ ", D. 4½ "

Empire period, mahogany and veneer case, acanthus-leaf and ring-carved attached pillars, spread eagle carving across top, house painted on lower glass; wooden works, weight-driven, coiled chime; white painted dial, flowers in spandrel corners, gilt chapter bands, time and strike. **(E)**

The National Museum of History and Technology, Smithsonian Institution

27-4 Column and Carved Splat Clock
Garner Curtis
Wolcottville, CT, c. 1828
H. 29 ", W. 17⅜ "

Empire period, Roman and Egyptian influences, wood veneer case with carved spread wing eagle splat, quarter columns carved in leaf design and paw feet, painted houses on lower section of door; 30-hour wood movement; white painted dial with gilt scrolls in spandrel corners, Arabic numerals, diamond-shaped hands, time and strike. On label "Made by Garner Curtis and sold by George D. Wadhams. Wolcottville, Connecticut." **(E)**

27-5 Column and Carved Splat Clock
Marsh, Gilbert and Company
Farmington, CT, c. 1829
H. 37 ", W. 17 ", D. 5 "

Empire period, Roman and Egyptian influences, walnut and veneer case, engaged carved columns, carved eagle and leaf top, mirrored door panel; 8-day movement; white painted dial with concentric gold circles and gold scrolls in spandrel corners, Arabic chapters, time and strike. **(E)**

Shelburne Museum, Inc.

27-6 Column and Carved Splat Clock
"Silas Hoadley Franklin Alarm"
Silas Hoadley
Plymouth, CT, c. 1830
H. 36", W. 17", D. 4½"

Empire period, mahogany veneer case, acanthus leaf, pineapple and ring-turned engaged columns, carved cornucopias arranged with fruit coming into center of splat, mushroom-shaped finials, mirror door; house, landscape, and pendulum bob oval painted on lower panel of door; wooden movement, ivory bushings; white painted dial with floral design in spandrel corners, Arabic chapters, time and strike. [Hoadley's geartrain was often called the "upside-down" movement because the winding drums and bell were at the top, and the escapement was at the bottom. On the "Franklin Alarm" label he often used Franklin's portrait and motto, "Time is Money."] **(E)**

The National Museum of History and Technology, Smithsonian Institution

27-7 Column and Carved Splat Clock
A. Munger & Company
Movement probably made by inmates of Auburn State Prison
Auburn, NY, c. 1833
H. 35", W. 16", D. 5"

Empire period, walnut veneer case, ebonized and gilt lower engaged columns, looking glass in lower door, hand-carved basket with fruit and leaves on splat, paw feet; 8-day brass movement; white painted, wood dial, Arabic chapters, diamond-shaped hands, brass second hand, time and strike. [Wallpaper on inside backboard and a flying eagle bob are characteristics of the Asa Munger clocks.] **(E)**

NAWCCM, Inc.

28 | Grecian Clocks

During the 1820s Joseph Ives, an ingenious clockmaker from Bristol, Connecticut, working in Brooklyn, New York, produced a wrought-brass strap movement with a unique spring lever system. This system required a clock case with a particularly wide base construction for the wide lever or wagon spring. It seems that three kinds of cases have been associated with this Ives movement, even though the cases of galleries and steeples were made to accommodate the invention. The first, found on the earliest "Brooklyn" model, was a half-round hollow-column case resting on a high and wide base. The second case included a set of large single turned volutes with brass centers resting on a wide base and supporting the large round brass dial frame and movement. It sat on small paw feet. In the early 1830s a third case appeared with its lever spring movement manufactured by Chauncey and Lawson Ives. It consisted of a wooden bezel, four turned wood volutes on a wide and high base ornamented with two columns, and ball feet. The two voluted cases—resembling the designs of Duncan Phyfe of New York, the leader of the early Empire school of chaste Greek furniture design and hence "Grecian"—have been attributed to the clock and cabinetmaker Elias Ingraham because they closely resemble the voluted or rosetted cases which he patented a few years later. Whether this handsome clock is called "Grecian," "Brooklyn," "Duncan Phyfe," or "Balloon," it represents a case form which was aesthetically pleasing to patrons of the nineteenth century and remains so today.

28-O Grecian Clock (color plate)
E. Ingraham & Company
Bristol, CT, c. 1871-83
H. 14½", W. 10¼", D. 4½"

Victorian period, classical influence, round rosewood case with carved volutes below dial frame, molded wood bezel, heavy wood base; 30-hour brass movement; white painted paper dial, moon-shaped hands, Roman chapters, time and strike. Case design patented March 31, 1868. Listed in 1880 catalogue for $5.25. On label "Elias Ingraham's Patent Sept. 30, 1862." **(F)**

NAWCCM, Inc.

28-1 Grecian Clock
"Duncan Phyfe," "Brooklyn Type"
Joseph Ives
Brooklyn, NY, c. 1826
H. 28⅜ ", W. 14 "

Empire period, classical influence, mahogany veneer on pine case, short black columns flanking a tall half-round column, mirrored base, brass ball feet, pewter bezel; 8-day wagon-spring wrought-brass strap movement; white painted dial, Roman chapters, time and strike. On dial "Joseph Ives, New York." **(E)**

American Clock & Watch Museum

28-2 Grecian Clock
"Brooklyn Type"
Joseph Ives
Brooklyn, NY, c. 1829
H. 33¾ ", W. 15¾ "

Empire period, classical influence, wood veneer case with gilded scrolled designs over dial and gilded spread-wing eagle at top, one set of large volutes with brass flower inset below dial; landscape, house, and pendulum bob oval painted on lower glass tablet; 8-day lever-spring brass movement with strap-brass design; printed paper dial pasted on wood, Roman chapters, time and strike. **(E)**

28-3 Grecian Clock
"Duncan Phyfe," "Brooklyn Type"
C. & L. C. Ives; Elias Ingraham, probably casemaker
Bristol, CT, c. 1830
H. 31¼ ", W. 16¼ "

Empire period, classical influence, rosewood veneer and black case, double set of volutes below movement, two landscape scenes painted in glass door panel, wood bezel; 8-day wagon-spring or patent lever, wrought-brass movement, time and strike. (Dial removed to show brass strap movement.) **(E)**

American Clock & Watch Museum

**28-4 Grecian Timepiece
"Balloon," "Alarm"
Seth Thomas Clock Co.
Thomaston, CT, c. 1900
H. 11", Dial 4"**

Victorian period, French Rococo influence, heavy cast-bronze case with ram's horn scrolls under dial, spread-wing owl under scrolls, on-off switch between dial and scrolls; one-day movement; white dial, separate second hand and dial, separate alarm hand and dial, Roman chapters, time only. On dial "Seth Thomas." **(F)**

B. C. & R. Roan, Inc.

**28-5 Grecian Clock
"Savoy Model"
Seth Thomas Clock Company
Thomaston, CT, c. 1909-10
H. 13¼", W. 7", D. 5", Base 6¾"**

Modern period, mahogany case with pressed inlay design, brass feet and bezel; 8-day spring-driven movement; white porcelain dial, Arabic chapters, slow-fast mechanism, spade hands, time and strike. **(F)**

The National Museum of History and Technology, Smithsonian Institution

29 | Ogee Clocks

The ogee clock case is a large rectangular late-Empire design featuring a wide "S"-molded or ogee-curved veneered surface stretching from the outer frame of the case to the frame of the inner door. It is this distinctive double-curved molding that gives the clock its name. When the ogee frame is flattened, creating an inclined frame, collectors call it a "beveled" case, even though the beveling removes the ogee curve. Nonetheless, some collectors still classify this non-ogee form as a "flat ogee." (The term "ogee," incidentally, appears frequently in horological literature as "O.G." and "ogive.")

Until recently, ogees were thought to have been first made in the early 1830s. But the labels on two ogees (if the labels are, in fact, original to the clocks) would seem to place the ogee design a decade earlier. One case bears a label marked "Chauncey Jerome." Since Jerome formed a new company with his brother and Elijah Darrow in 1827, the label indicates that the clock was made prior to 1827. The other case bears a label marked "George Marsh/ Winchester, Conn." If it refers to the same George Marsh who bought a clock shop with William Gilbert in 1828, then this ogee dates back at least to 1828.

Ogee cases were designed as moderately-priced cases meant to house simple weight-powered movements. Brooks Palmer believes that the Chauncey and Nobel Jerome ogee with a cheap one-day weight-powered brass movement revived the clock industry after the Panic of 1837. In 1841 Brewster and Kirk equipped ogees with spring-driven movements. The simplicity of the design made ogees among the most versatile of clock cases.

29-O Ogee Clock (color plate)
F. C. Andrews
New York, NY, c. 1845
H. 27¾", W. 16¾", D. 4¼"

Victorian period, classical influence, mahogany case, "S"-shaped molded frame, vase of flowers and architectural panel painted on lower glass panel; 8-day weight-driven brass movement; white painted dial, Roman chapters, time and strike. On label "Patent/Brass Clocks,/Made and Sold by F. C. Andrews,/New York/[and] Directions for Setting . . . Running and keeping it in Order. . . ." Label printed by S. Folsom, Hartford. **(F)**

Irvin G. Schorsch III

29-1 Ogee Clock
George Marsh
Winchester, CT, c. 1828
H. 25", W. 5", D. 4¼"

Empire period, classical influence, walnut veneer case, vase of three flowers with classical figures standing on columns painted on lower glass tablet; 30-hour weight-driven brass movement; white painted iron dial with painted flower in each spandrel corner, raised chapter ring, Roman chapters, time and strike. On label "Improved Thirty Hour/Brass Clocks/Made and Sold by/George Marsh,/Winchester, Conn." Label printed by Herald Job Press, Winsted, CT. **(F)**

Irvin G. Schorsch III

29-2 Ogee Clock
Chauncey Jerome
Bristol, CT, c. 1838
H. 27", W. 14"

Victorian period, classical influence, "S"-shaped molded frame case, flowers and rectangular leaf border painted on lower glass panel; one-day brass movement; white painted dial, leaf and flower motifs in spandrel corners, Roman chapters, time and strike. Marked inside "Chauncey Jerome." **(F)**

The National Museum of History and Technology, Smithsonian Institution

29-3 Ogee Clock
Forestville Manufacturing
Company
Bristol, CT, c. 1839
H. 30¾", W. 17", D. 4¼"

Empire period, mahogany veneer ogee molded case, crossed-leaf design painted on lower glass panel; 8-day brass weight-driven movement; white painted wood dial with flowers painted in spandrel corners, Roman chapters, time and strike. On dial and stamped on movement "Forestville Mfg. Co./Bristol, Ct. U.S.A." On label "Improved/Eight Day/Brass/Clocks./Made and Sold by Forestville Manufacturing Co./Bristol, Ct. . . . Warranted if Well Used." Label by "Huyler & Rickey Book and Job Printers." **(F)**

Irvin G. Schorsch III

29-4 Ogee Clock
Boardman & Wells
Bristol, CT, c. 1840
H. 26", W. 15½", D. 4½"

Victorian period, classical influence, walnut veneer case; 30-hour brass weight-driven movement; white painted wood dial with floral sprig in spandrel corners, brass alarm ring in center, Roman chapters, time, strike, and alarm. On label "Extra Clocks /Made and Sold by Boardman & Wells/Bristol, Conn . . . /Elihu Geer, Job and Card Printer, Hartford." **(F)**

Private Collection

29-5 Ogee Clock
Henry C. Smith
Plymouth, CT, c. 1840
H. 26½", W. 15½", D. 4¾"

Victorian period, classical influence, rosewood ogee-molded case; 8-day pendulum movement; white painted iron dial with flowers in spandrel corners, Roman chapters, time and strike. On label "Extra/ Clocks/Manufactured by/Henry C. Smith./Plymouth, Conn.,/and Sold Wholesale and Retail/Joseph Hurlbut, Printer, Hartford." **(F)**

29-6 Ogee Clock
Maker unknown
CT, c. 1840
H. 26", W. 15½", D. 4½"

Victorian period, mahogany veneer case with etched glass; 30-hour brass weight-driven movement; white painted iron dial with floral spray in spandrel corners, raised chapter ring, Roman chapters, time and strike. **(F)**

Private Collection

29-7 Ogee Clock
Birge, Mallory & Company
Bristol, CT, c. 1840
H. 26", W. 15¾", D. 4¼"

Victorian period, classical influence, mahogany veneer case; 30-hour unbeaded brass-strap movement; white painted and gilt wood dial, gilt spandrel corners, Roman chapters, time and strike. On label "Thirty Hour Clocks Manufactured by/Birge, Mallory & Co./Bristol, Conn./and Sold Wholesale and Retail. . . ." **(F)**

29-8 Ogee Timepiece
Seth Thomas Clock Company
Plymouth, CT, c. 1840
H. 31½"

Victorian period, classical influence, "S"-shaped molded pine case; vase and flowers in oval surround painted on lower glass tablet; 8-day pendulum movement; white painted dial, raised chapter ring, Roman chapters, time only. Maker and place stamped on movement. **(F)**

29-9 Ogee Clock
Clarke, Gilbert & Company
Winchester, CT, c. 1841
H. 25¾", W. 15½", D. 4½"

Victorian period, classical influence, mahogany and veneer case, etched glass tablet; 30-hour weight-driven movement; white painted dial, raised chapter ring, purple flowers in spandrel corners, Roman chapters, time and strike. On label "Patent/Brass/Clock/Made and Sold by/Clarke, Gilbert & Co./Winchester, Conn. . . . Huyler & Rushey Knickerbocker Printing Office, N.Y." **(F)**

The National Museum of History and Technology, Smithsonian Institution

29-10 Ogee Clock (variation) "Bevel Case"
Daniel M. Tuthill
Saxtons River, VT, c. 1842
H. 26", W. 15¾", D. 4¾"

Victorian period, classical influence, tiger maple and mahogany case; 30-hour wooden movement with brass bushings in front plate only; white painted wood dial, gilt in spandrel corners, Roman chapters, time and strike. On label "Extra improved brass-bushed clocks manufactured and sold, wholesale and retail by D. M. Tuthill, Saxton's River, Vt., 1842." Label printed by Moore of Vermont. **(F)**

NAWCCM, Inc.

29-11 Ogee Clock
William S. Johnson
New York, NY, c. 1845
H. 26", W. 15¾", D. 4¼"

Victorian period, classical influence, mahogany veneer case, green background and flower basket painted on glass tablet; brass movement; white painted wood dial, gilt in spandrel corners, Roman chapters, time and strike. On label "William S. Johnson/... D. Murphy Book & Job Printer, N.Y." **(F)**

NAWCCM, Inc.

29-12 Ogee Clock
J. C. Brown, Forestville Mfg. Company
Forestville, CT, c. 1850
H. 26", W. 15¼", D. 4¼"

Victorian period, wood veneer case, clear glass panel; 30-hour brass weight-driven movement; separate wind hole in dial at 6 for alarm; white painted dial, separate brass alarm ring, design painted in spandrel corners, Roman chapters, time, strike and alarm. **(F)**

29-13 Ogee Clock
Waterbury Clock Company
Waterbury, CT, c. 1857
H. 26 ", W. 17 ", D. 3¼ "

Victorian period, classical influence, walnut veneer case, roses painted on lower glass panel; 30-hour brass weight-driven movement; white painted iron dial, Roman chapters, time and strike. On label "Waterbury Clock Co./Waterbury, Conn./Manufacturers of/Eight Day and Thirty Hour/ Brass Clocks and Timepieces./ Also Regulators in every style." **(F)**

Private Collection

29-14 Ogee Clock
Seth Thomas Clock Company
Plymouth Hollow, CT, c. 1863
H. 26 ", W. 15½ ", D. 4½ "

Victorian period, classical influence, maple and rosewood veneer case, view of Boston painted on glass tablet; 30-hour weight-driven movement; white painted metal dial, raised chapter ring, time and strike. On label "Brass Clocks Made and Sold by Seth Thomas, Plymouth Hollow, Conn. . . ." Label printed by Elihu Geer, Hartford. Listed in 1863, 1868, 1869 catalogues. **(F)**

NAWCCM, Inc.

29-15 Ogee Clock
E. N. Welch Manufacturing
Company
Forestville, CT, c. 1864
H. 26 ", W. 15¼ ", D. 4 "

Victorian period, classical influence, rosewood case, "View of/ St. George's Edinburgh" painted on lower glass panel; improved 30-hour brass weight-driven movement; white painted metal dial with blue flowers in spandrel corners, Roman chapters, time and strike. On label "Improved Thirty Hour Brass Clocks Made and

Sold by the E. N. Welch Mfg. Co.,
Forestville, Conn./Calhoun, Printers, Hartford, Conn." **(F)**

Private Collection

30 | Steeple (Sharp Gothic) Clocks

In 1845, three years after Robert Connor published **The Cabinet-maker's Assistant**, the first design book on Gothic Revival furniture published in the United States, Elias Ingraham made his first sharp Gothic steeple clock. After the heavy carving and gilding of the Empire period, the chaste cathedral-like case must have been a welcome relief. It held single and double sets of steeples flanking the sharp Gothic top and it came in four sizes—the subminiature at 10½-inches high, the miniature at 14¾-inches high, the standard at 20-inches high, and the double steeple at 23½-inches high. The steeples resembled cones, candlesticks, or ring-turned finials. The clock with four steeples on one level was called a four-steepled clock or a steeple-on-base. The clock with tiered steeples was called a steeple-on-steeple or double-steeple clock.

According to Paul R. de Magnin, writing in the National Association of Watch and Clock Collectors **Bulletin** of 1967, certain generalizations can be drawn about the steeple form. It usually has a metal dial with a triangular top to fit into the pine and mahogany-veneer case. The finials or steeples are of solid wood, and a decorative scene like Saratoga Springs, the White House, the New York coat of arms, Trafalgar Square, Port of Havana, flying eagles, balloons, geometric or floral motifs usually ornament the lower glass tablet. A wood strip between the dial glass and glass tablet signals that the clock is an early form. The Maltese Cross is a familiar design for the hands. Seth Thomas, however, used "S" and "T" for his dial hands.

The steeple case is a versatile design. Although it basically housed brass spring-driven thirty-hour time-and-strike movements, it also housed Silas B. Terry's eight-day coiled-spring balance-wheel movement, and his thirty-hour time movement. Some cases included alarm components, fusees, and weights. The steeple-on-steeple was sufficiently large to contain the Ives eight-day wagon or "accelerating lever spring" movement. The calendar mechanism was popular in the steeples manufactured between 1875-80.

Although the Gothic furniture style never gained great acceptance in America—perhaps because it was too regal and imposing in a case piece, chair, or bed—the steeple clock remained a favorite among manufacturers like Ingraham, Jerome, Forestville, Gilbert, Ansonia, Boardman, Thomas, and Birge & Fuller. It remains aesthetically pleasing today.

3O-O Steeple Clock (color plate, left)
"Double Steeple," "Steeple-on-Steeple"
Theodore Terry and Franklin C. Andrews
Bristol, CT, c. 1842-50
H. 25", W. 12¾", D. 4½"

Victorian period, Gothic influence, rosewood veneer case, two tiers of conical steeples, two glass painted panels—the lower, a fountain and birds, the upper an eagle with banner and arrows similar to eagle printed on label inside; 8-day brass spring movement; white painted metal dial, raised chapter ring, Roman chapters, time and strike. On label "Made and Sold by/Terry and Andrews, Bristol, Conn. . . . Patent Spring Brass Eight Day Clocks" **(F)**

Steeple Clock (color plate, right)
"Sharp Gothic"
Ansonia Brass Company
Ansonia, CT, c. 1854
H. 19¾", W. 9¾", D. 3¾"

Victorian period, Gothic influence, rosewood veneer case, set of turned steeples, bird and cherry branch painted on glass panel; 30-hour brass spring-driven movement; white painted metal dial, moon-shaped hands, Roman chapters, time and strike. On label "Eight Day and Thirty Hour O.G. & OO.G. With and Without Alarms, Gothic, Spring, . . . Sharp & Round Top . . . Marine Lever Timepiece, for Ships, Steamboats, Locomotives, and Dwellings, Octagon Eight Day Clocks, Silent and Striking, for Hotels and Offices . . . Ansonia Brass Co., Ansonia, Conn . . . Benlam, Steam Printer, New Haven." **(F)**

Irvin G. Schorsch III

3O-1 Steeple Clock
"Sharp Gothic"
Chauncey Boardman and Col.
Joseph A. Wells
Bristol, CT, c. 1838
H. 20", W. 9½", D. 3½"

Victorian period, Gothic influence, mahogany veneer, cherry sprig painted on glass panel; white painted dial, raised chapter ring, Roman chapters, time and strike. On label "Equalizing and Retaining Spring/Brass Clocks/ Warranted Good if Well Used/ Made and Sold by C. Boardman, Also by J. A. Wells/Bristol, Conn./ Springs being . . . manufactured by the most celebrated Spring Maker in the City of New York." **(E)**

Private Collection

30-2 Steeple Clock
"Double Steeple" or "Steeple-on-Steeple"
John Birge and Thomas Fuller
Bristol, CT, c. 1845
H. 27"

Victorian period, Gothic influence, mahogany case, four bun feet, four tiered conical steeples on plinths, two doors with birds painted on middle glass panel and geometric design on lower panel; wagon-spring movement, invented by Joseph Ives; white painted dial, raised chapter ring, Roman chapters, time and strike. **(D)**

Index of American Design, National Gallery of Art, Washington

30-3 Steeple Clock
"Four Poster"
John Birge and Thomas Fuller
Bristol, CT, c. 1845
H. 20"

Victorian period, Gothic influence, mahogany veneer case with four trumpet-shaped steeples on columns on raised, curved plinths; two doors, bun feet, middle and lower glass panels decorated with fern-like design applied by decalcomania; wagon-spring movement; white painted dial, raised chapter ring, Roman chapters, time and strike. **(D)**

Index of American Design, National Gallery of Art, Washington

30-4 Steeple Clock
"Single Steeple" or "Sharp Gothic"
Elisha Brewster and Elias Ingraham
Bristol, CT, c. 1845
H. 19⅞", W. 8¾", D. 3⅝"

Victorian period, Gothic and classical influences, walnut veneer and glass case; molded sides resembling half-round columns, curved Gothic top molding, slightly turned gilded steeples, gilded ball feet, harbor scene painted on glass tablet; brass driving spring; white painted dial, Roman chapters, time and strike. On dial "Brewster & Ingraham/Bristol, CT. U.S." On label "Patent Spring Brass Clocks Made and Sold by Brewster & Ingraham, Bristol, Conn." **(F)**

The National Museum of History and Technology, Smithsonian Institution

30-5 Steeple Clock
"Double Steeple," "Candlestick," "Wagon Spring"
Birge & Fuller
Bristol, CT, c. 1844-48
H. 21"

Victorian period, Gothic and classical influence, walnut veneer and glass case, wide base houses wagon-spring movement, four candlestick steeples (two on each side) on Empire-molded curved bases flanking central case with sharp Gothic top, middle and lower glass tablets painted in floral and fern design, ball feet; leaf spring connected by chain to small diameter of compound pulley, large diameter of compound pulley connected by cord to 8-day wagon-spring movement; white painted dial, Roman chapters, time and strike. **(D)**

The National Museum of History and Technology, Smithsonian Institution

30-6 Steeple Clock
"Double Steeple," "Steeple-on-Steeple"
Birge & Fuller
Bristol, CT, c. 1844-48
H. 27½"

Victorian period, Gothic influence, rosewood veneer case, painted glass panels, conical double-tiered steeples; 8-day movement; white painted dial, Roman chapters, time and strike. **(E)**

Robert W. Skinner, Inc.

30-7 Steeple Clock
"Single Steeple" or "Sharp Gothic"
Theodore Terry and Franklin C. Andrews
Bristol, CT, c. 1842-50
H. 19", W. 10", D. 4½"

Victorian period, Gothic and classical influences, mahogany veneer case, half-round engaged columns, one pair of steeples, sharp Gothic top, glass panel painted and gilded in floral and leaf design; 8-day brass movement, coiled chime, alarm attachment and bell; plate-pressed sheet metal dial painted white, alarm ring in open center around hand arbor, Roman chapters, time and strike. On label "Made and sold by Terry and Andrews, Bristol, Conn." **(F)**

The National Museum of History and Technology, Smithsonian Institution

30-8 Steeple Timepiece
"Four Poster"
Brewster and Ingrahams
Bristol, CT, c. 1844-52
H. 19 ", W. 10½ ", D. 3½ "

Victorian period, Gothic influence, rosewood veneer case with molded Gothic top, two sets of free-standing columns and two sets of ring-turned steeples, pastoral scene painted on lower glass panel; 8-day brass spring-driven movement; white painted metal dial, Roman chapters, time only. On label ''Brass Clocks,/Warranted not to fail. Made and Sold by/Brewster & Ingrahams/Bristol, Conn.'' **(E)**

Private Collection

30-9 Steeple Clock
"Four Poster," "Round Gothic," "Rippled"
Elias Ingraham, case designer
Forestville Manufacturing Company
Forestville, CT, c. 1848
H. 19½ ", W. 12 "

Victorian period, Gothic influence, wood case with four free-standing columns and turned candlestick finials; carved rippled wood bezel, base, and round Gothic top; the White House, the Potomac River, and sailboat painted on glass tablet; 8-day spring movement; white painted dial, Roman chapters, time and strike. **(F)**

30-10 Steeple Clock
Silas B. Terry
Terryville, CT, c. 1848
H. 24½ "

Victorian period, Gothic and classical influences, wood veneer case, one set of conical finials, painted lower tablet; 8-day spring balance wheel (marine) control movement; white painted metal dial, separate second hand and dial, opening in lower dial allows oscillations of the balance wheel to be seen, Roman chapters, time and strike. **(E)**

30-11 Steeple Clock
"Sharp Gothic"
Atkins Clock Company
Bristol, CT, c. 1859
H. 19½", W. 9½", D. 3¾"

Victorian period, Gothic influence, rosewood veneer case, one pair of turned steeples on plinths, Gothic top and sides with heavy molding, eagle with banner and American flag painted on blue glass tablet; 30-hour brass spring-driven movement; white painted metal dial, Roman chapters, time and strike. On label "Thirty Hour/Clock and Time pieces/Made and Sold by the/Atkins Clock Company/Bristol, Ct./J. B. Page, Printer, Hartford, Ct." **(F)**

Private Collection

30-12 Steeple Clock
Atkins Clock Company
Bristol, CT, c. 1860
H. 19½", W. 9¾"

Victorian period, mahogany case with turned finials, painted glass panel below dial; two-train movement; white painted dial, Roman chapters, time and strike. **(F)**

31 | Acorn Clocks

One of the most prized clocks today is the so-called "acorn." It was made essentially by one man, J. C. Brown, and by the Forestville Manufacturing Company in Bristol, the name of his firm after 1848. With the exception of minor changes in the formation of the top from round to rounded Gothic and in the arms which followed the curvilinear case lines instead of becoming columns and finials, it resembled the Ives hourglass model, another prize in the world of clock collecting.

In his cases Brown used the innovative technique of laminating woods which the famous German cabinetmaker of New York, John Henry Belter, had introduced to American Rococo Revival furniture design four years earlier. Brown tipped his wooden side arms with acorn finials and placed the case on a low wooden base or on French tapered feet reminiscent of the thin Hepplewhite pillar and scroll form. His glass tablets were painted with scenes depicting the Connecticut State House in Hartford, the Merchants' Exchange in Philadelphia, and Brown's own house, among others, as well as floral scrolled patterns and other simple painted motifs. Brown devised an eight-day brass time-and-strike fusee spring movement for the case. Without one of the chief technological advancements of the period, however—coiled steel springs—his acorn shape would not have been possible.

31-O Acorn Clock (color plate)
J. C. Brown, designer
Forestville Manufacturing Company
Bristol, CT, c. 1845
H. 24½″, W. 14½″

Victorian period, Gothic and Rococo influences, mahogany veneer and glass case; house, trees, lake, and sailboat painted on glass, small oval for viewing pendulum movement, round Gothic top suggests acorn shape, side brackets capped by acorn finials follow serpentine sides of case; white painted dial, Roman chapters, time and strike. On dial "Forestville Manuf. Co. Bristol, Ct., U.S.A." **(B)**

Old Sturbridge Village, Inc.

31-1 Acorn Clock (variation)
"Hourglass"
Joseph Ives
Plainville, CT, c. 1840
H. 24″, W. 14½″

Victorian period, classical and French influences, mahogany and veneer case with free-standing columns replacing the usual acorn side arms, two wood urn-shaped finials, landscape design painted on glass tablet; 30-hour brass movement; brass dial, raised chapter ring, Roman chapters, time and strike. **(B)**

31-2 Acorn Clock (variation)
"Hourglass"
Joseph Ives
Plainville, CT, c. 1840
H. 23″

Victorian period, classical and French influences, mahogany and veneer case with free-standing columns replacing the usual acorn side arms, two wood urn-shaped finials, tall columned church and triangular-shaped pendulum bob window painted on glass tablet; one-day wagon-spring movement; dial has Roman chapters, time and strike. On label "Plainville, Conn." **(B)**

31-3 Acorn Clock
J. C. Brown, designer
Forestville Manufacturing Company
Bristol, CT, c. 1845
H. 23½", W. 13¾"

Victorian period, Gothic and classical influences, mahogany veneer case with harbor scene, scrolls, and pendulum bob oval painted on glass tablet; laminated wood side brackets capped with wooden acorn finials; white painted dial, Roman chapters, time and strike. **(B)**

Israel Sack, Inc., N.Y.C.

31-4 Acorn Clock
J. C. Brown, designer
Forestville Manufacturing Company
Bristol, CT. c. 1845
H. 24", W. 14"

Victorian period, Gothic and classical influences, mahogany veneer case with painting of the Merchants' Exchange in Philadelphia on glass, acorn-shaped top in rounded Gothic form, laminated wood side brackets capped with wooden acorn finials; glass around dial painted with oak leaves, small flowers, and lyre motifs in three upper corners similar to design on Aaron Willard's Massachusetts Shelf Clock (see 19-0); 8-day brass movement, main springs in base of clock, wood fusees in front of each spring; white painted dial, Roman chapters, time and strike. On dial "Forestville Manuf. Co./Bristol, Ct. U.S.A." On glass panel "Merchants' Exchange/Philadelphia" **(B)**

Greenfield Village and Henry Ford Museum

31-5 Acorn Clock
J.C. Brown
Forestville, CT, c. 1849
H. 19¼", W. 10¾"

Victorian period, Gothic and classical influences, wood veneer case without side brackets, glass around dial painted in red and gold with lyre motifs in three corners, lower glass panel decorated with one large painted lyre; eight-day fusee spring-powered movement; white painted dial, raised chapter ring, Roman chapters, time and strike. [This model without side brackets was likely the last in the series of Acorns made by J.C. Brown.] **(B)**

32 | Skeleton Timepieces

By the middle of the eighteenth century, French masters like Pierre Le Roy and Ferdinand Berthoud had devised timekeepers (very much resembling medieval clocks) in which the entire mechanism, displayed under glass domes, could be viewed and enjoyed. The plates of these movements were narrow so that the wheels and all brassy surfaces could shine through to the viewer. By the early nineteenth century, these skeleton timekeepers were produced in England and America. The beauty of Silas Terry's American skeleton timepiece (32-1) is certainly a consequence of his ability to handle brass and to realize in three dimensions the inherent architectural beauty of machinery.

No one knows exactly why exposed movements came into fashion in the 1850s. But one can hardly question the relationship between this vogue and the new industrial age, an age that increasingly put its faith in technological knowledge and on practical truths to ease life and to elicit eternal and universal truths. The Victorians came to appreciate the complexity of mechanical activity, to recognize the glory of function, to see beauty in the way a thing worked. Victorian families were also enthusiastic collectors of mundane oddities. The skeleton timepiece, consequently, like china ornaments, wax fruit, and stuffed birds, enjoyed its proper place in the parlor, unmoving and under glass.

32-O Skeleton Timepiece (color plate)
Irenus Atkins, manufacturer
Joseph Ives, patentee of movement
Bristol, CT, c. 1860
H. 20", W. 13¼", D. 7½"

Victorian period, experimental case and movement, glass dome; 30-day wagon-spring movement; engraved, silvered, pierced dial, Roman chapters, time only. On dial "Irenus Atkins, Bristol, Conn." **(D)**

W. G. Harding

32-1 Skeleton Timepiece
Silas Burnham Terry
Terryville, CT, c. 1845
H. 20"

Victorian period, experimental clock, glass dome instead of case, marble and wood base, penny feet; brass movement, balance wheel escapement; white painted iron dial, sweep second hand, Roman chapters, time only. **(D)**

Old Sturbridge Village, Inc.

32-2 Skeleton Timepiece
Silas Burnham Terry
Terryville, CT, c. 1850
H. 11"

Victorian period, wooden base with wooden bun feet holding exposed movement; brass dial, separate counterbalanced second hand, Roman chapters, time only. **(D)**

33 | Iron-Front Clocks

Innovative materials like innovative designs titillated the imaginations of the Victorian buyers of American clocks. At the end of the 1840s James Bogardus of New York introduced the architectural profession to the possibilities inherent in cast-iron building materials. By 1855 cast iron had been adapted to garden bench and chair designs, and by 1857 iron was being cast in molds and assembled into clock cases.

C. and N. Muller of New York manufactured the popular iron cathedral-shaped and figured cases which were used by the Waterbury, Jerome, and American clock companies. Sometimes iron-front cases, decorated with mother-of-pearl inlay and gilded or painted in scrolled designs, resembled the French Rococo scroll-footed china and papier-mâché boudoir clocks which were also being manufactured in great quantities by 1860 (see section 34).

Iron fronts, stylized to suggest medieval and Gothic façade as well as to revive classical cupid-like creatures in the curvilinear French style, represented the mid-Victorian interest in simulating the "educated European look" at home. Clockmakers were as enthusiastic about their particular abilities to incorporate such cultivated taste in their work as they were in employing innovative American machine designs. In a cooperative exchange, they provided furniture designers with coiled metal springs, which had come from the timekeepers' movements and which the designers quickly applied to the making of comfortable spring-supported chairs; and the furniture designers in turn provided the latest American interpretation of high-style case piece patterns from Europe.

33-O Iron-Front Timepiece (color plate)
"Kossuth"
American Clock Company
New York, NY, c. 1865
H. 20", W. 18¾", D. approx. 4½"

Victorian period, French and Egyptian influences, iron-front case, brass bezel, glass in pendulum bob opening with brass bezel, gilt hoof feet, roses and gilt scrolls painted over case and in center of dial; white painted metal dial, Roman chapters, time only. Stamped on movement "Pat'd May 10, 1859." **(F)**

William Penn Memorial Museum, Pennsylvania Historical and Museum Commission

33-1 Iron-Front Clock
Chauncey Jerome
New Haven, CT, c. 1845-55
H. 15¼", W. 10½", D. 4"

Victorian period, Gothic influence, black painted cast-iron cathedral facade with wood box for movement, mother-of-pearl inlay, round glass for pendulum bob; 30-hour spring-driven brass movement; white painted dial, Roman chapters, time and strike. Stamped on movement "Chauncey Jerome/New Haven/Conn. USA." **(F)**

NAWCCM, Inc.

33-2 Iron-Front Clock
"Lion Head"
The American Clock Company
New York, N.Y., c. 1850
H. 15½", W. 10½", D. 4"

Victorian period, Egyptian influence, gilt metal front and wood case, round pendulum bob glass; 30-hour movement with brass plates, steel springs; white painted dial, Arabic chapters, time and strike. On label "Manufactured and Sold by the American Clock Company." **(F)**

NAWCCM, Inc.

33-3 Iron-Front Clock
"Cupid"
U.S. Clock Company, Manufacturer
Nicholas Muller, casemaker
New York, NY, c. 1850
H. 15½", W. 13", D. 3½"

Victorian period, Baroque influence, cast-metal case with cupids and grapes, round pendulum bob glass; 30-hour brass movement; white painted dial, Roman chapters, time and strike. On dial "U.S. Clock Company/ New York." **(F)**

NAWCCM, Inc.

33-4 Iron-Front Clock
Chauncey Jerome
New Haven, CT, c. 1850
H. 16", W. 8", D. 3¼"

Victorian period, Rococo influence, iron front and pine box, round pendulum bob opening in facade; spring-driven movement; white painted tin dial, Roman chapters, time and strike. On movement "Chauncey Jerome, New Haven, Conn. U.S.A." **(F)**

Philip H. Bradley Co.

33-5 Iron-Front Clock
Elias and Andrew Ingraham
Bristol, CT, c. 1852
H. 16¾"

Victorian period, Rococo influence, cast-iron case, mother-of-pearl inlay, gilt scrolls border case as well as inner frame of door, floral design on lower glass panel; 8-day spring-driven movement; white painted metal dial, Roman chapters, time and strike. On dial "E. & A. Ingraham, Bristol/Ct." **(F)**

Greenfield Village and Henry Ford Museum

33-6 Iron-Front Clock
Patented by C. Chinnocks
Possibly made by Terhune & Botsford
Possibly New York, NY, c. 1854
H. 10¼", W. 12¼", D. 4¾"

Victorian period, Gothic influence, cast-iron case, iron half-round engaged columns ending in steeples with Gothic tops, three fleur-de-lis finials, facade resembles a cathedral, painted scene under dial with mother-of-pearl insets, pendulum bob opening in base; white painted metal dial, Roman chapters, time and strike. Cast inside "C. Chinnocks' Patent Applied For." **(F)**

William Penn Memorial Museum, Pennsylvania Historical and Museum Commission

33-7 Iron-Front Clock
American Clock Company
Bristol, CT, and New York, NY, c. 1855
H. 19", W. 14", D. 3½"

Victorian period, mahogany painted metal case, French-type scroll front feet, painted scene below dial; 8-day spring movement; white painted metal dial, Roman chapters, time and strike. **(F)**

33-8 Iron-Front Clock
Maker unknown
Probably American, c. 1858
H. 16½", W. 14¾", D. 3½"

Victorian period, French Rococo influence, iron front and pine case, molded and painted cast-iron flowers and butterflies on facade, pendulum bob glass with metal bezel below dial; white painted dial, Roman chapters, time and strike. **(F)**

Mahlon L. Jacobs

33-9 Iron-Front Timepiece
"Cupid"
W. S. Johnson, manufacturer or retailer
Nicholas Muller, case maker
New York, NY, c. 1860
H. 19"

Victorian period, classical influence, cast-iron case with three cupids surrounding dial, round pendulum bob window below dial; spring movement; white dial, Roman chapters, time only. **(F)**

33-10 Iron-Front Clock
"Mother and Child"
Nicholas Muller
New York, NY, c. 1880
H. 17½", W. 15½", D. 4½"

Victorian period, metal case with mother and child, egg and dart molding across top of clock cornice, scroll feet, draped metal garlands; 30-hour brass movement; white painted dial, Roman chapters, time and strike. **(F)**

NAWCCM, Inc.

33-11 Iron-Front Clock
"Evangelist"
Waterbury Clock Company, manufacturer
Nicholas Muller, case maker
Waterbury, CT and New York, NY, c. 1890
H. 19½"

Victorian period, Gothic influence, cast-iron front, round pendulum bob window below dial, two evangelists on either side of window; spring movement; white painted dial, Roman chapters, time and strike. **(F)**

---

34 | Porcelain and Papier-Mâché Clocks

Mid-nineteenth-century papier-mâché and porcelain cases seem to have been especially designed for use in the bedroom. Almost always fashioned in the Rococo Revival style, they were ornate and often decorated with delicate mother-of-pearl inlay. Like other small and fashionable clocks of their day, they were powered by cheap coiled springs and balance wheels, which allowed the process of miniaturization to take place. Because these clocks boasted spring-driven mechanisms, they were the descendants of the eighteenth-century English bracket clock and the early nineteenth-century Heman Clark double-decker.

The technological innovations of a few American clockmakers helped to lay the foundations for the small movements of porcelain and papier-mâché clocks. Silas Burnham Terry discovered a cost-cutting method of producing temper-coiled springs in 1830. In 1838 Joseph Shaylor Ives designed a mechanism to convert weight-driven movements to spring-driven ones. In 1840 John Pomeroy developed a tempering process which made a smooth and easier surface on which to work when making the movements. And, finally, clockmakers found that they could use local steel instead of the expensive brass material in the construction of springs.

Papier mâché is, of course, a medium consisting of pressed pulp or strips of paper in glue. The molded papier-mâché form, treated with coats of heavy (and often black) lacquer was then painted and gilded. Papier-mâché clock cases seem either to have been made in Litchfield, Connecticut or to have been imported from England. Samuel N. Botsford made many of the high-grade movements used with papier-mâché cases. The watch escapements of Sully and Enderlin are also found in some eight-day and thirty-hour Litchfield papier-mâché cases, assembled and marketed by the Jerome Manufacturing Company.

The porcelain cases called "Beleek" were made in the 1890s at the Willets Manufacturing Company and at the Ott and Brewer Company of Trenton, New Jersey. Royal Bonn porcelain imported from Germany by the Ansonia and the E. N. Welch companies housed both thirty-hour and eight-day movements.

34-O Porcelain Clock (color plate)
Ansonia Clock Company
New York, NY, c. 1890
H. 10", W. 8"

Victorian period, Royal Bonn porcelain table clock; 8-day movement;

porcelain dial, Roman chapters, time and strike. Printed on dial "Mfd. by Ansonia Clock Co., N.Y., U.S.A." **(F)**

Lorretta Marder Interiors

34-1 Papier Mâché Clock
Maker unknown
Litchfield Manufacturing Company, case maker
Litchfield, CT, c. 1852
H. 25¾", W. 21¼"

Victorian period, French influence, papier mâché case with paint, mother-of-pearl inlay and scrolled feet on decorated base; 8-day movement; white painted dial, Roman chapters, time and strike. **(F)**

34-2 Papier Mâché Timepiece
Jerome Manufacturing
**   Company**
S. N. Botsford, movement
**   designer**
New Haven, CT, c. 1853
H. 11½", W. 8", D. 5½"

Victorian period, French Rococo influence, papier mâché case with gilt, sea shell, and mother-of-pearl inlay; 30-hour marine or lever movement; hair-spring balance; white painted dial, Roman chapters, time only. On label "Botsford Improved/ Patent Lever Marine Time Piece." **(F)**

NAWCCM, Inc.

34-3 Porcelain Timepiece
E. N. Welch Manufacturing
**   Company**
Bristol, CT; Hamburg, Germany,
**   c. 1870**
H. 19", W. 16", D. 8"

Victorian period, Gothic influence, decorated ceramic architectural case in brilliant blues, greens, and yellows (case probably made in Germany); 30-hour movement; white dial, Roman chapters, spade hands, separate second hand and dial, time only. **(F)**

NAWCCM, Inc.

34-4 Porcelain Timepiece
Waterbury Clock Company
Waterbury, CT, c. 1891
H. 6″, W. 4¼″, D. 2″

Victorian period, French Rococo influence, white ceramic case with gilt and floral decoration, brass bezel; 30-hour lever escapement; white paper dial, scrolls in center, Arabic chapters, separate second hand and dial, slow-fast mechanism, time only. On back "Waterbury Clock Co. U.S.A." Patent May 6, 1890; Dec. 23, 1890; Jan. 13, 1891. **(F)**

NAWCCM, Inc.

34-5 Porcelain Timepiece
"Boudoir"
Waterbury Clock Company
Waterbury, CT, c. 1895
H. 7″

Victorian period, French Rococo influence, porcelain case with stylized French scrolled feet, hand-colored floral decorations; one-day movement; white painted dial, Arabic chapters, separate second hand and dial, time only. Listed in 1895 Montgomery Ward & Company catalogue for $2.30 **(F)**

34-6 Porcelain Clock
Waterbury Clock Company
Waterbury, CT, c. 1902
H. 11½″, W. 9½″, Dial 4½″

Victorian period, French and Egyptian influences, imported French porcelain case, gilded and painted in green floral design, four paw feet; steel spring movement; ivory-finish dial, Arabic chapters, time and strike with cathedral gong. Listed in 1902 Sears, Roebuck & Co. catalogue for $6.15. **(F)**

34-7 Porcelain Timepiece
"The Dainty"
Waterbury Clock Company
Waterbury, CT, c. 1902
H. 5½″, W. 6″, dial 2″

Victorian period, French Rococo influence, porcelain case with gilt and paint, scroll feet; one-day lever movement; white dial, Arabic chapters, separate second hand and dial, time only. Listed in 1902 Sears, Roebuck & Co. catalogue for $1.60. **(F)**

**34-8 Porcelain Clock
"La Mosella"
Ansonia Clock Company,
    manufacturer
New York, NY, c. 1914
H. 12½", W. 10¾", D. 5"**

Modern period, French Rococo influence, Royal Bonn decorated-ceramic case with scroll feet, asymmetrical leaf design at top, flower of pink and purple painted on case, green paint outlines, brass bezel; 8-day metal movement; egg and dart molding around white porcelain dial, Roman chapters, time and strike. On dial trademark and "Manufactured by the Ansonia Clock Company, New York, United States of America." **(F)**

NAWCCM, Inc.

35 | Calendar Clocks (Shelf)

In the 1850s clockmakers devised a calendar timekeeper that within a decade could be purchased comfortably by the average family. Catering to the curiosity inherent in human nature, the calendar clock satisfies the quest for a knowledge about things by providing semi-scientific information—the hour of the day, day of the week, day of the month, month of the year, the phase or age of the moon, and, more rarely, the time of high and low tides. In a day long before electronic communication, long-range planning was considerably enhanced by this shelf-size instrument.

Although many of the fine movements and a few of the plainer movements in eighteenth-century tall-case clocks contained day-of-the-month mechanisms, patents for separate calendar clock movements were not registered until about 1853. In the early '60s the Seth Thomas Clock Company bought the patents of the Mix brothers and made calendar clocks with double dials separating the time-telling dial from the calendar dial. For a little style and appeal the company ornamented some with patriotic designs.

The Ithaca Clock Company also made double-dial time, strike, and calendar clocks, which it boxed in elegant parlor cases designed with architectural tops and well-turned finials. After 1865 the Ithaca company specialized in calendar movements, and by 1881 companies like Waterbury issued catalogues with a section devoted entirely to the Ithaca calendars, which could be "furnished with months and days of the week in the English, Spanish, Portuguese, French, German, Russian and Asiatic Languages."

Silas Burnham Terry, the great clock mechanic known for his tempered-steel springs, received a patent in 1868 for a single-dial brass-movement calendar clock. It was produced the following year by the Ansonia Brass and Copper Company. A few calendar clock designers used both black and white dials, the black showing the day and month; the white showing the time. Cases varied in style from box to column, to round, to pedimented, to partial octagon, and finally to cabinet (gingerbread). Most were designed to hold brass movements and continued to be popular until 1910 or so. Today calendar clocks are among the most avidly collected of all timekeepers.

35-O Calendar Clock (color plate)
"Parlor Model"
Ithaca Calendar Clock Company, manufacturer
H. B. Horton, patentee of calendar movement
Ithaca, NY, c. 1870
H. 20¾", W. 10½", D. 5½"

Victorian period, classical and Baroque influences, walnut case, ebony pediment and carving, cut glass pendulum; glass calendar dial with silver Arabic numerals, silver and black time dial with Roman chapters, time, strike, day, date, and month. On calendar dial "H. B. Horton's Patents April 18, 1866 and August 28th, 1866. Ithaca Calendar Clock Co., Ithaca, N.Y." **(D)**

W. G. Harding

35-1 Calendar Clock
Seth Thomas Clock Company
Plymouth Hollow, CT, c. 1860
H. 30¼", W. 18½", D. 5"

Victorian period, Empire influence, rosewood veneer case with octagonally-cut engaged columns with cut bases, painted on middle glass tablet gold eagle holding American flag with 33 stars; spring movement; white painted upper dial, Roman chapters, time and strike; white lower dial, Arabic numerals, day, date, and month. **(D)**

35-2 Calendar Clock
Ithaca Calendar Clock Company
Ithaca, NY, c. 1866
H. 23", W. 12", D. 5¾"

Victorian period, Empire influence, rosewood case with stylized columns and three turned wood finials; spring movement; white painted, upper time dial, Roman chapters, time and strike; white lower dial, Arabic numerals, day, date, and month. On lower dial "Manufactured by/The/Ithaca Calendar Clock Co./Ithaca, N.Y." **(D)**

35-3 Calendar Clock
"Parlor Calendar"
Ithaca Calendar Clock Company
Ithaca, NY, c. 1866
H. 19"

Victorian period, Queen Anne influence, black walnut case on case with columns on upper case and carved design across arched top; spring movement, glass pendulum bob; black painted upper dial, white Roman chapters, time and strike; black lower dial with Arabic numerals, day, date, and month. On lower dial "Ithaca Calendar Clock Co." **(D)**

35-4 Calendar Clock
"Parlor Calendar No. 1"
Seth Thomas Clock Company
Thomaston, CT, c. 1868
H. 20", W. 12¾", D. 5¼"

Victorian period, Empire influence, rosewood case, large wood moldings around dials, slightly arched top, plinth-type base; 8-day weight-driven brass movement of the "Lyre" design, calendar unit; white painted metal upper dial, Roman chapters, time and strike; white painted lower dial, day, date, and month. On movement "S. Thomas/Plymouth, Conn./U.S.A." **(D)**

NAWCCM, Inc.

35-5 Calendar Clock
Ithaca Calendar Clock Company
Ithaca, NY, c. 1868
H. 22¾", W. 11½", D. 4"

Victorian period, wood veneer case with half-round molding across top; 8-day spring movement; white painted upper dial with separate brass alarm ring in center, Roman chapters, time, strike and alarm; white lower dial with Arabic numerals, day, date, and month. On lower dial "H. B. Horton's/Patent . . . Ithaca Calendar Clock Co./Ithaca, N.Y." **(D)**

35-6 Calendar Clock
"Fashion No. 3"
The Southern Calendar Clock
Company
Seth Thomas Clock Company,
maker of dead-beat and
calendar mechanisms
St. Louis, MO, and Thomaston, CT,
c. 1879-89
H. 32", W. 16", D. 5¾"

Victorian period, Queen Anne influence, stained oak case with
free-standing columns on side,
arched top with three turned finials, molded base; 8-day spring-
driven movement, dead-beat escapement, perpetual calendar
mechanism; white painted metal
upper dial, Roman chapters, separate second hand and dial with
Arabic numerals; white painted
metal lower dial, Arabic numerals
indicating day, date and month;
time and strike. On upper dial
"Patented Dec. 28, 1875." On
middle of glass case in gilt
"Fashion." On lower dial "Southern Calendar/Clock Co./St. Louis,
Mo./Patented March 18th 1879."
(D)

NAWCCM, Inc.

35-7 Calendar Clock
"No. 8, Shelf Library"
Ithaca Calendar Clock
Company
E. N. Welch, movement maker
B. B. Lewis, patentee of "club
foot" escapement
Ithaca, NY, c. 1875
H. 25½", W. 12", D. 4½"

Victorian period, Chippendale influence, walnut-stained oak case,
arched top, single wood finial;
brass movement; white painted
metal upper dial, Roman chapters; white painted metal lower
dial, day, date, and month; time
and strike. On lower dial "H. B. Horton's/Patents/April 18, 1865 and
August 28, 1866/Ithaca Calendar
Clock Co./Ithaca, N.Y." **(D)**

NAWCCM, Inc.

35-8 Calendar Clock
New Haven Clock Company
New Haven, CT, c. 1885
H. 21¼", W. 11", D. 5¼"

Victorian period, Oriental influence, press-molded oak case; 8-day movement with calendar mechanism actuated by lever; white paper upper dial, wood bezel, date and month; white painted lower dial, metal Roman chapters, brass bezel; time and strike. **(F)**

NAWCCM, Inc.

35-9 Calendar Clock
"Arditi"
E. N. Welch Mfg. Co.
Daniel Jackson Gale, patentee of perpetual calendar movement
Forestville, CT. 1895
H. 27⅛", W. 17", D. 5¾"

Victorian period, Oriental influence, press-molded oak with machine-molded fretwork, brass bezels; 8-day and calendar movement; white paper upper dial with Roman chapters; lower dial has two separate hands and dials within the larger date dial, Arabic numerals giving day, date, and month; time and strike. **(F)**

NAWCCM, Inc.

---

36 | Blinking Eye Timepieces

The "Winkers"—the animated timepieces patented in 1857 by Pietro Cinquini of West Meriden, Connecticut, and assigned to art metal-goods manufacturers Nathaniel Bradley and Walter Hubbard, were made as sixteen- to seventeen-inch cast-iron models of literary, political, and animal figures popular in the 1860s and '70s. Among these figures were the Continental Soldier also called "Toby," John Bull also called the "Squire," St. Nicholas, Topsy, Sambo, the Organ Grinder, the Lion, and the Spaniel Dog. Bradley and Hubbard purchased thirty-hour brass movements for the figures from Seth Thomas or the Waterbury clock companies. According to Fred and Mary Fried in America's Forgotten Folk Art, **the cast-iron figures were** hand painted at the factory by women who worked by the piece instead of by the hour. Another group of figures, made flat instead of dimensionally, were the Lewis Carroll characters, the Knave and the White Rabbit, from the memorable Alice in Wonderland.

The movements in these cast-iron figures are regulated by short bob pendulums with both dial and movement inserted into the stomach of each figure. The movement drives the eyes of the soldier and the squire, for example, in a vertical or up-and-down direction, and the eyes of the Carroll figures from side to side in a horizontal direction. The side-to-side movement is also typical of contemporary Black Forest animated timepieces. Some of the Bradley and Hubbard figures also contain automated alarms. Their "winkers" contain reasonably good balance wheel movements.

36-0 Blinking Eye Timepiece (color plate, left)
"Sambo"
Waterbury Clock Company
Waterbury, CT, c. 1870
H. 16"

Victorian period, cast-iron enameled case; heavy 30-hour balance-wheel lever escapement movement; white painted dial, Roman chapters, time only. Listed in later (1875) catalogue for $5.75. **(E)**

W. G. Harding

Blinking Eye Timepiece (color plate, right)
"Topsy, Winter"
Waterbury Clock Company
Waterbury, CT, c. 1870
H. 17¼"

Victorian period, cast-iron enameled case, heavy, 30-hour, balance-wheel, lever escapement movement; eyes move vertically when clock is running; white painted dial, Roman chapters, time only. Listed in later (1875) catalogue for $5.75. **(E)**

W. G. Harding

36-1 Blinking Eye Timepiece
"Hessian Soldier," "Toby," or
   "Winker"
Bradley & Hubbard, maker
Petro Cinquini, designer
Chauncey Jerome, probable
   movement maker
Meridan, CT, c. 1857
H. 16⅝", W. 10⁷⁄₁₆", D. 7⅞"

Victorian period, cast-iron figure with tricorn hat and buckled shoes, dial and movement placed in stomach of figure; eyes move up and down with each oscillation of balance wheel and verge, 30-hour brass lever move-

ment; white dial, Roman chapters,
slow-fast mechanism, time only.
Patented July 14, 1857. **(E)**

The National Museum of History
and Technology, Smithsonian Institution

36-2 Blinking Eye Timepiece
"Continental," "Toby," "Winker"
Bradley & Hubbard Manufactur- ing Company
Petro Cinquini, designer
Chauncey Jerome, movement maker
Meriden, CT, c. 1857
H. 17", W. 7½", D. 5"

Victorian period, cast-iron figure
with tricorn hat and buckled
shoes, dial and movement in
stomach of figure, eyes move up
and down with oscillation of balance wheel and verge; 30-hour
brass lever movement; white
painted dial, Roman chapters,
slow-fast mechanism, time only.
Stamped on movement "C.
Jerome." [Figure identical with
36-1, but paint colors completely
different.] **(E)**

NAWCCM, Inc.

36-3 Blinking Eye Timepiece
"John Bull," "Toby," "Winker," "Squire"
Bradley & Hubbard Manufactur- ing Company
Petro Cinquini, designer
Chauncey Jerome, movement maker
Meriden, CT, c. 1860
H. 16", W. 9", D. 6"

Victorian period, cast-iron figure
painted in brown, green, red and
white; dial and movement in
stomach of figure, eyes move vertically with oscillation of balance
wheel, brass bezel; 30-hour brass
lever movement; white painted

dial, Roman chapters, slow-fast mechanism, time only. Stamped on movement "C. Jerome." **(E)**

NAWCCM, Inc.

36-4 Blinking Eye Timepiece "The White Rabbit"
Attributed to Terry Clock Company
Probably Waterbury or Winsted, CT, c. 1870
H. 12 ", W. 5½ ", D. 3 "

Victorian period, cast-metal painted figure on wooden stand, character from Lewis Carroll's Alice in Wonderland (1865); 30-hour brass movement, small anchor (3 tooth span), short bob pendulum moves eyes horizontally unlike iron Winkers; white painted dial, Roman chapters, time only. **(E)**

NAWCCM, Inc.

36-5 Blinking Eye Timepiece "The Knave"
Attributed to Terry Clock Company
Probably Waterbury or Winsted, CT, c. 1870
H. 11½ ", W. 5½ ", D. 2¾ "

Victorian period, cast-metal painted figure on wooden stand, character from Lewis Carroll's Alice in Wonderland (1865); 30-hour brass movement, small anchor (3 tooth span), short bob pendulum moves eyes horizontally unlike iron Winkers; white painted dial, Roman chapters, time only. **(E)**

NAWCCM, Inc.

37 | Round Tops

Throughout the nineteenth century, shelf clocks continued to diminish in size, and they could be purchased in a variety of styles and shapes, including small cases with flat, round, or pedimented tops. The round-topped shelf clock was sometimes only ten-inches high. Although it was made by manufacturers like Elisha Brewster, William Gilbert, Ansonia Brass, and Seth Thomas, the round-top case was most often associated with Elias Ingraham, who made a large part of his fortune from the small classical model listed in his catalogue as "Venetian." Ingraham enjoyed using "ancient" names for his products, and clock historians have noted that he had great financial success with his "Venetian," "Doric," "Grecian," and "Ionic," designs. Common to almost all Ingraham models are a set of volutes below the time dial.

When made of wood, the round-top clock usually has a double dial, and sometimes a double door. The lower door contains a decorated glass instead of the clear glass used when a calendar dial is behind it. Round-top cases without volutes were made by Elisha Brewster. But the same maker also produced round-tops with volutes and these clocks occasionally contain a "tinplate" movement patented by Joseph Ives in 1859 and manufactured by Noah Brewster. The voluted Brewster round-top clock has a two-sectioned wooden frame door and volutes between the two glass panels. It resembles the volute placement of Ingraham's "Grecian," "Doric," and "Ionic" models.

Other round-tops were made of iron with single dials and single, small glass panels. These could be bought with either eight-day or thirty-hour movements.

37-O Round Top Clock (color plate)
"Tudor, No. 3"
Seth Thomas Clock Company
Thomaston, CT, c. 1870
H. 12", W. 8¼", D. 4", Dial 4"

Victorian period, rosewood veneer case; 8-day spring-driven brass movement; white painted metal dial with flowers in center, spade hands, Roman chapters, time and strike. On label "Spring Brass Eight Day Clocks; Half Hour Strike . . . Seth Thomas Cl. Co./Thomaston/Connecticut." Listed earlier in 1863 catalogue; discontinued in 1881. **(F)**

NAWCCM, Inc.

37-1 Round Top Clock
Eagle Manufacturing Company
Chauncey Jerome, movement maker
Possibly Portsoken, England (case) and Bristol, CT (movement), c. 1850
H. 14¾", W. 9¾", D. 4¼"

Victorian period, classical influence, burled walnut case; 8-day brass movement; white dial, Roman chapters, moon-shaped hands, time and strike. **(F)**

NAWCCM, Inc.

37-2 Round Top Clock
"Arcadian"
Ansonia Brass & Clock Company
Ansonia, CT, c. 1860
H. 19", W. 11½"

Victorian period, classical influence, mahogany veneer case, half-round columns called split spindles, molded base, floral painting on glass tablet; 8-day movement; white painted dial, Roman chapters, time and strike. **(F)**

Index of American Design, National Gallery of Art, Washington

37-3 Round Top Clock
"Venetian"
Probably E. Ingraham Co.
Bristol, CT, c. 1860
H. 18"

Victorian period, classical influence, mahogany and glass case, half-round columns called split spindles, volutes between upper and lower glass dials typical of Ingraham design; 8-day movement; white painted dial, Roman chapters, time and strike. **(F)**

Index of American Design, National Gallery of Art, Washington

37-4 Round Top Clock
"Venetian"
E. Ingraham & Company
Bristol, CT, c. 1865
H. 15″

Victorian period, rosewood case, wood bezels, volutes separating upper and lower dials, lower dial painted with clover design; one-day spring movement; white painted dial, Roman chapters, time and strike. **(F)**

37-5 Round Top Timepiece
"Venetian"
E. Ingraham & Company
Bristol, CT, c. 1865
H. 13¾″, W. 9¼″, D. 4¼″

Victorian period, classical influence, rosewood veneer case with volutes and engaged split spindle columns, green and gilt scrolled design on lower glass door; 8-day brass spring-driven pendulum movement; white paper dial, time only. On label "E. Ingraham & Co." [Dial removed to show mechanism.] **(F)**

NAWCCM, Inc.

37-6 Round Top Clock
Terry Clock Company
Waterbury, CT, c. 1868
H. 8⅛″

Victorian period, round-top black iron case, brass bezel; one-day spring movement; white painted dial, Roman chapters, time and strike. **(F)**

37-7 Round Top Timepiece
Terry Clock Company
Waterbury, CT, c. 1869
H. 6", W. 4¼", D. 2½", Dial 6"

Victorian period, Empire influence, black metal case, brass bezel; one-day movement; white dial, brass alarm ring, moon-shaped hands, Roman chapters, time and alarm. Patented Dec. 1, 1868 and Apr. 27, 1869. **(F)**

NAWCCM, Inc.

37-8 Round Top Clock
Terry Clock Company
Waterbury, CT, c. 1869
H. 8", W. 5½", D. 3", Dial 8"

Victorian period, Empire influence, black painted metal case on plinth; one-day movement; white dial, Roman chapters, brass alarm ring in center, moon-shaped hands, time, strike, and alarm. On back label "The Terry Clock Co./Patent/One-day/Time-Pieces/Alarm Time-Pieces/and/Striking Clocks, with or without Alarms/Patented Dec. 1, 1868, and May 4, 1869." **(F)**

NAWCCM, Inc.

37-9 Round Top Clock
Chelsea Clock Company
Boston, MA, c. 1900
H. 16", W. 7⅛"

Victorian period, round-top mahogany case with small ball feet, brass bezel; 8-day spring-driven movement with balance wheel; white painted dial, Arabic chapters, slow-fast mechanism at top of dial, time and ship bell strike. On dial "Chelsea" **(F)**

38 | Pedimented Tops

The development of the tempered coiled spring, which Silas Terry patented in 1830, allowed Ingraham, Thomas, and others more freedom in designing small cases. No longer needing room for the dropping of weights, casemakers could cater to the American taste for novel and inexpensive decorative elements by making minor changes in the "roof-line" of the clock. The suggestion of a pitched or gabled roof on a straight-sided, unshaped body of a clock, a roof otherwise described as being of a modified Gothic style, was initiated in 1860 by Elias Ingraham. Here was another double-dial small case with carved volutes separating the dial frames. This clock Ingraham labeled "Doric," suggesting the straight, columnar sides and pedimented roof line of the oldest and simplest of the classical architectural orders.

A variation on Ingraham's "Doric" or gabled roof was the partial octagon or hexagon top, resembling the many-sided hanging gallery and schoolhouse cases made by the Welch, Atkins, New Haven, Jerome, S. B. Terry, and Waterbury clock companies. Other cases with four-sided tops were made by the Ithaca Calendar Clock Company. Seth Thomas sold many three-sided or partial hexagon top models with the inner dial frames correspondingly slanting on the sympathetic sides, and Gilbert made a pedimented alarm clock with a small looking-glass panel and a thick rosewood base. As a group these clocks might best be called "pedimented tops," an easy form of classification according to the essential "architectural" shape of their roofs.

38-0 Pedimented (Gabled) Clock (color plate)
"Doric"
E. Ingraham & Company
Bristol, CT, c. 1871
H. 16", W. 8", D. 3¾", Dial 5½"

Victorian period, classical influence, rosewood case with engaged gilt split-spindle columns; double dial (the lower only painted glass) and pair of volutes separating dials; white painted dial, Roman chapters, time and strike. On label "Eight Day and One Day Brass Clock . . . Trade Doric Mark . . . Elias Ingraham's Patent,/Sept. 3^d, 1861/Renewed Sept. 3^d, 1868,/Patented March 30th, 1869,/Mosaic Front/ Patented June 6, 1871/E. Ingraham & Co./Warranted Superior. Bristol, Conn./Calhun Printing Works, Hartford." **(F)**

NAWCCM, Inc.

38-1 Pedimented (Partial Octagon) Clock
American Clock Company
New York, NY, c. 1850
H. 15¼", W. 10½", D. 4½"

Victorian period, Gothic influence, rosewood veneer case, gilded around door frame, flowers and scrolls painted on glass tablets; brass movement; white painted metal dial, Roman chapters, time and strike. **(F)**

NAWCCM, Inc.

38-2 Pedimented (Partial Hexagon) Clock
Seth Thomas
Plymouth, CT, c. 1860
H. 9", W. 5¾"

Victorian period, wood veneer case, molded sides and top, black and gilt design painted on lower glass tablet; 30-hour movement, off-center pendulum; white painted, metal dial, separate brass alarm ring, Roman chapters, time, strike, and alarm. **(F)**

38-3 Pedimented (Partial Hexagon) Clock
Seth Thomas Clock Company
Plymouth Hollow, CT, c. 1863
H. 14½", W. 8", D. 3"

Victorian period, rosewood veneer, black paint and gilt on glass panel; 30-hour spring-driven brass movement; white painted metal dial, raised chapter ring, Roman chapters, S and T hands, time and strike. On label "Seth Thomas Plymouth Hollow, Connecticut." **(F)**

38-4 Pedimented (Gabled) Time-piece
Maker unknown
Probably CT, c. 1865
H. 11¾″, W. 7¾″, D. 3¾″

Victorian period, rosewood veneer case, gold and red design on painted black glass tablet, gilt edges around two glass panels; spring-driven movement; white painted iron dial, Roman chapters, time only. Stamped on back "Watch & Clockmakers, Jewelers, Cutlers, Opticians & c . . . Kegg's Stores 28 & . . . High St . . . Kings V[ille?]" **(F)**

Private Collection

38-5 Pedimented (Gabled) Timepiece
Seth Thomas Clock Company
Thomaston, CT, c. 1890
H. 11½″, W. 9″

Victorian period, wood case, unusual fretwork with silk backing behind fretwork in upper portion of case; 30-hour movement; painted dial, time only. "S.T." inscribed on movement. **(F)**

Lorretta Marder Interiors

38-6 Pedimented (Partial Octagon) Clock
"Parlor Calendar No. 5"
Seth Thomas Clock Company
Thomaston, CT, c. 1875
H. 20¼″, W. 13″, D. 5¼″

Victorian period, walnut-stained oak case with small volutes (left one as door handle) between upper and lower glasses, one door, lower clear glass allows day and month rollers to be seen turning; 44E movement; white painted metal dial, Roman chapters, spade hands, time and strike.

[Lower dial removed to show mechanism.] **(F)**

NAWCCM, Inc.

38-7 Pedimented (Gabled) Clock
"Doric"
E. Ingraham & Company
Bristol, CT, c. 1880
H. 16½", W. 10½", D. 4¾"

Victorian period, Gothic influence, wood veneer case, molded sides and molded gabled top, wood bezels, volutes separating upper and lower dials, lower glass painted in geometric designs; 8-day movement; white painted dial, Roman chapters, separate glass alarm ring in center, time, strike, and alarm. **(F)**

38-8 Pedimented (Partial Octagon) Clock
"Doric," "Mosaic"
E. Ingraham & Company
Bristol, CT, c. 1874
H. 16", W. 9"

Victorian period, Grecian influence, wood case, wood bezels, volutes separating upper and lower dials, lower glass painted in floral design; 8-day spring movement; white painted dial, Roman chapters, time and strike. **(F)**

39 | Carriage Clocks

The American carriage clock was derived from the seventeenth-century English coach watch (sometimes as large as seven inches in diameter), from the English spring-driven bracket clock, and from the French design called the "pendule de voyage." Like each of its predecessors, it was intended for serious travelers to carry in leather cases and to hang in carriages or tavern rooms. It gave travelers a sense of the time while in public places, and, if it contained alarm components, it lessened the chances of being late. By the time this rectangular brass-and-glass timekeeper had become popular and plentiful in America, carriage travel had greatly diminished. Railroads, of course, now provided the traveler with a dynamic new means of transportation, and public regulator timepieces kept the travelers and the railroads on time. Carriage clocks after 1880 became decorative ornaments retaining once-functional brass handles as a reminder of their original portable nature.

Although the English manufactured a few fine carriage clocks, French clockmakers, in particular, specialized in elegant, portable models. The Americans copied the French. The Waterbury Clock Company was the most prolific of the American manufacturers of carriage clocks, New Haven, Seth Thomas, Welch, and Jerome each putting out similar models, almost all of them cheap reproductions. The Joseph Eastman, Boston, Chelsea, and Vermont clock companies, however, produced excellent American carriage clocks with sturdy, carefully aligned cases and brass finishes almost as fine as the French originals. In his book, **Carriage Clocks: Their History and Development,** Charles Allix writes that when a French carriage clock was cheap it had the very worst kind of platform cylinder escapement, but when the Americans made a cheap clock, they still used a lever (though pin-pallet) escapement. The essential flaw in America's cheap cases rests with the fast assemblage and pressed, stamped sheet-brass materials which were not worth repairing and gave the Americans the reputation for creating the first "throw-aways" of the nineteenth century.

Although carriage clocks look basically alike, the manufacturers made certain that the names of their models were very different, if not fanciful. The Waterbury Clock Company patented a one-day time-and-alarm model called the "Traveler" in 1881. Ansonia put out a model called "Peep O'Day" in 1877 and another they called "Climax" in 1886. The New Haven Clock Company, like other manufacturers, occasionally produced carriage clocks for organizations. (Its 1912 model for the Elks has "New York Lodge No. 1" inscribed on the dial.) Waterbury made the "Hornet," "Guide," "Speck," and "Conductor," models between 1887 and 1890, and the "Wanderer" and "Sage" in the first decade of the twentieth century.

39-O Carriage Timepiece (color plate)
Ansonia Clock Company
New York, NY, c. 1890
H. 5½", W. 4"

Victorian period, ornate gilded metal case and handle, beveled glass on four sides; 8-day lever spring movement; enameled dial, time only. Printed on dial "Mfd. by the Ansonia Clock Co. New York, U.S.A."
(F)

Lorretta Marder Interiors

39-1 Carriage Timepiece
Waterbury Clock Company
Waterbury, CT, c. 1878
H. 4¾", W. 3", D. 2"

Victorian period, classical influence, brass case and handle, incised work below dial; brass movement; white dial, spade hands, Roman chapters, time only. On dial "Pat. May 21. 1878." **(F)**

NAWCCM, Inc.

39-2 Carriage Clock
"Carriage Extra"
Ansonia Clock Company
New York, NY, c. 1880
H. 7½", W. 5", D. 3½", Dial 2½"

Victorian period, classical influence, nickel plated with top handle and bracket feet; steel spring lever escapement; white dial, spade hands, Arabic chapters, slow-fast mechanism, separate second hand and dial, time, strike, and alarm. On back plate trademark and "Ansonia Clock Co." **(F)**

NAWCCM, Inc.

39-3 Carriage Timepiece
Ansonia Clock Company
New York, NY, c. 1880
H. 4½"

Victorian period, brass case, beveled glass on four sides, stylized bracket feet and handle on top; spring lever movement; white porcelain dial, Arabic chapters, time only. **(F)**

39-4 Carriage Timepiece
Seth Thomas Clock Company
Thomaston, CT, c. 1880
H. 4¼", W. 3¼", D. 2"

Victorian period, classical influence, enameled black-metal square case with brass handle and bezel; 8-day brass movement; white dial spade hands, Arabic chapters, slow-fast mechanism, time only. On dial "8 day/Made by Seth Thomas in U.S.A." **(F)**

NAWCCM, Inc.

39-5 Carriage Timepiece
Waterbury Clock Company
Waterbury, CT, c. 1880
H. 5¾"

Victorian period, brass case with stylized bracket feet and handle, pressed case design; spring lever movement; white dial, separate second hand and dial, Roman chapters, time and alarm. **(F)**

39-6 Carriage Clock
Waterbury Clock Company
Waterbury, CT, c. 1890
H. 5⅝", W. 3", D. 2½"

Victorian period, classical influence, brass case and handle, glass sides; spring movement; white painted metal dial, spade hands, Roman chapters, time and strike (hour and half-hour). **(F)**

NAWCCM, Inc.

39-7 Carriage Clock
"Guide"
Waterbury Clock Company
Waterbury, CT, c. 1901
H. 7", W. 4½", D. 3¼", Dial 2¾"

Victorian period, classical influence, silvered and brass case with handle and glass sides; 8-day movement; white dial, spade hands, separate second hand and dial, Roman chapters, time and strike (hour and half-hour). On dial "Manufactured by Waterbury Clock Co. U.S.A." Patented Dec. 6, 1887, Mar. 19, 1889, Jan. 13, 1891, Jan 29, 1901. **(F)**

NAWCCM, Inc.

39-8 Carriage Timepiece
"Junior Tattoo"
New Haven Clock Company
New Haven, CT, c. 1904
H. 4½", W. 3¼", D. 2¼"

Modern period, classical influence, rectangular brass case, handle, and bracket feet; 8-day movement; white dial, Arabic chapters, spade hands, separate second hand and dial, time and alarm. On dial "New Haven/ Junior Tattoo" and "The New Haven Clock Co. U.S.A." **(F)**

NAWCCM, Inc.

39-9 Carriage Timepiece
"Bonnibel"
Ansonia Clock Company
Ansonia, NY, c. 1914
H. 5¼", W. 3", D. 2½"

Modern period, classical influence, brass case, handle, and bracket feet, four sides of beveled glass; 8-day movement; white porcelain dial, Roman chapters, spade hands, time only. On dial "Mfg'd by The Ansonia Clock Co./ New York, U.S.A." and trademark. **(F)**

NAWCCM, Inc.

40 | Crystal Regulators

The preference of nineteenth-century French clockmakers for recti-linear glass and brass-trimmed forms evident in the carriage clock is also reflected in the crystal regulator, a variation of the carriage clock with four glass sides. The typically classical ten-inch columned case with an enameled dial, circular movement, dead-beat escapement, and compensated pendulum usually incorporating two small vials of mercury was initially a precision striking instrument as well as an object of considerable artistic endeavor.

Ansonia and Waterbury clock companies produced American versions of the fashionable glass regulator. The more expensive models maintained precision elements, and the cheaper models offered the mere "aspect" of a crystal Regulator, the "look" of mercury-filled cylinders if not the actual presence of any real pendulum compensating factor. Although most American regulators had flat brass tops and modified bracket feet, a few were fashionably designed with Japanese pagoda-shaped tops and Rococo-Revival scrolled feet. To the pleasure of owning a beautiful case were added the pleasures of viewing its works—of observing the passage of time, the mysteries of control, and the intrigue of the machine at work.

40-0 Crystal Regulator Clock
"Elysian"
Ansonia Clock Company
New York, NY, c. 1914
H. 16", W. 8", D. 4½"

Modern period, classical influence, gilded metal and glass case; 8-day brass, visible jeweled Brocot escapement, simulated mercury compensated pendulum; white enameled dial, slow-fast mechanism, spade hands, Arabic chapters, time and strike. On dial "Manufactured by the Ansonia Clock Co. New York, United States of America." **(F)**

NAWCCM, Inc.

40-1 Crystal Regulator Clock
Seth Thomas and Sons
Thomaston, CT, c. 1868
H. 12¼", W. 9¼", D. 5½"

Victorian period, classical influence, brass and glass case, four free-standing reeded columns, 8-day brass-spring simulated mercury pendulum movement; white porcelain dial decorated with rose garland, slow-fast mechanism, Arabic chapters, time and strike. [Glass-sided French-type shelf clock listed in 1868 catalogue.] **(E)**

Private Collection

40-2 Crystal Regulator Clock
Seth Thomas and Sons
Thomaston, CT, c. 1868
H. 15", W. 8"

Victorian period, Oriental influence, pagoda-top glass and gilded metal case, four beveled glass panels, stylized bracket feet; imitation mercury pendulum, 8-day movement; white porcelain dial, time and strike. On dial "Seth Thomas." [Listed in 1868 catalogue.] **(E)**

Loretta Marder Interiors

40-3 Crystal Regulator Clock
Seth Thomas and Sons
Thomaston, CT, c. 1870
H. 12"

Victorian period, classical and Empire influences, glass and brass case with free-standing glass columns decorated with gold enamel floral motifs, gilt ball feet; 8-day brass spring pendulum movement; white porcelain dial, Roman chapters, time and strike. On dial "Seth Thomas." **(E)**

Robert Skinner, Inc.

40-4 Crystal Regulator Clock
William L. Gilbert Clock
Company
Winsted, CT, c. 1871
H. 9½", W. 6½", D. 5¼"

Victorian period, classical influence, rectangular metal and glass flat-topped case, thick base and stylized bracket feet; outside escapement, pendulum hangs behind large spring; white porcelain dial, Arabic chapters, eagle-type hour hand, time, strike, and alarm. **(E)**

Mr. & Mrs. Charles H. Gale

40-5 Crystal Regulator Clock
Boston Clock Company
Chelsea, MA, c. 1880
H. 24½", W. 8", D. 6¼"

Victorian period, pagoda top, French-type feet, cast-metal and glass case; tandem wind compensated balance wheel movement which requires only one winding arbor for both time and strike; the strike train winds by turning the key one way, the time train by turning it the other way; white porcelain dial with garland ornamenting inner circle, spade hands, slow-fast mechanism, Arabic chapters, time and strike. **(F)**

NAWCCM, Inc.

40-6 Crystal Regulator Clock
Waterbury Clock Company
Waterbury, CT, c. 1886
H. 10¼", W. 5¼", D. 4¼"

Victorian period, Empire influence, metal and glass case with curved arch and ball feet; movement and pendulum exposed to view, outside escapement, pendulum hangs in front of large spring; white porcelain dial, Arabic chapters, time, strike, and alarm. On dial "Manufactured by Waterbury Clock Co., U.S.A." **(E)**

Mr. and Mrs. Charles H. Gale

40-7 Crystal Regulator Clock
Chelsea Clock Company
Chelsea, MA, c. 1900
H. 10", W. 6¼", D. 4¾"

Victorian period, classical influence, brass and glass case, brass bezel; balance escapement movement; white enameled metal dial, spade hands, Arabic chapters, time and strike. On dial "A. Stowell & Co. Inc./Boston" (retailers). **(F)**

NAWCCM, Inc.

41 | Globe Timepieces

New York spawned the short-lived but stimulating educational tool, the time globe. According to Theodore R. Timby, the inventor of this mechanism in 1863, the object of the timepiece was "to arrange a terrestrial globe in such a relation to a dial plate and index that the culminating time of the sun, and consequently the true solar time, and also the clock or mean time, can be observed simultaneously at any moment."

Another time-globe, made by Lewis P. Juvet of Glenn's Falls, New York, was described, in 1877 as "A universal time-keeper . . . [giving] longitude and latitude of any place in the world, as well as the difference of the same between two or more places. It stands in any position without injury to the works, has no more pieces in its construction than an ordinary watch and is a stem winder." The address of the Reverend Russell A. Olin to the National Educational Association in Washington in 1880 proclaimed the virtues of these time globes to teachers in the public schools and colleges. "Wonderfully simplifying the principles of practical Geography," he exclaimed, the time globe enables librarians and teachers to extend the comprehension of students to include time at different places on the earth all at once.

Although Juvet's factory, built with partner James Arkell in 1879, burned and was never rebuilt again, his time globe, as well as Timby's solar timepiece was a significant achievement that combined the quest for geographical knowledge with the nineteenth century's fondness for mechanical invention.

41-O Globe Timepiece (color plate)
"Solar Timepiece," "Improved Solar Time-Globe"
Theodore R. Timby, inventor; Lewis E. Whiting, manufacturer; Gilman Joslin, globemaker
Baldwinsville and Saratoga Springs, NY and Boston, MA, c. 1865
H. 27", W. 15"

Victorian period, walnut case, molded arch top, ringed finial, drop wood acorn below molded outer edge; 12-hour dial above globe (globe more decorative than functional when compared with the Juvet time globe, 41-1), minutes dial in base below, time only. **(D)**

American Clock & Watch Museum

41-1 Globe Timepiece
"Time Globe"
Louis P. Juvet, inventor
Louis P. Juvet and James Arkell, manufacturers
Glens Falls, NY
Invented 1867, manufactured 1880-86
H. 18" (model came in various sizes)

Victorian period, globe which revolves by a clock mechanism with sliding Vernier divided in 360 degrees indicating latitude, longitude, and time in any place in the world. **(D)**

Private Collection

41-2 Globe Timepiece
Laport Hubbell
Bristol, CT, c. 1870
H. 24½", W. 14"

Victorian period, Gothic influence, triple-peaked cathedral facade case on high base, gilded wood ball representing the sun in center of facade; 8-day movement with globe below upper dial; lower dial has white painted face, Roman chapters, time only. [Limited number produced.] **(D)**

41-3 Globe Timepiece (above)
"Terrestrial Globe Timepiece"
Globe Clock Company, manufacturer
Laport Hubbell, marine movement
Milldale and Bristol, CT, c. 1883
H. 17", Diam. 13"

Victorian period, table-variety globe on Empire-style marble stand, balance escapement, brass movement. **(D)**

American Clock & Watch Museum

42 | Figured Mantel Clocks

Although clocks incorporated into the design of sculpture had long been popular on the Continent, particularly in France, a vogue for heavy bronze figured mantel clocks did not become widespread in America until the 1880s at the height of a period now frequently called "high-Victorian." In parlors and drawing rooms that boasted heavily carved Renaissance Revival furniture, arbiters of Victorian taste dictated accessories that complemented this stylistic return to an earlier day. Just as the Classical Revival had made high fashion of carved marble busts borrowed from Greek and Roman sources, the late Victorians doted on bronze figural sculpture executed in what they liked to think of as the "Olde English" style. These romantic figures—frequently of medieval knights or French cavaliers, ancient heroes like Hercules and Cincinnatus, and actual or literary personages like Shakespeare or Don Juan—were employed in high-Victorian interiors in many ways: as free-standing sculpture, as elaborate decoration for newel posts, and especially as figured mantel clocks.

While many of the more expensive figured mantel clocks included the timekeeper in its overall design, many others were merely common blacks (see section 45) with a bronze sculpture—frequently of a horse, stag, or dog—added to its flat top. Many makers, like Ansonia, sold their blacks with or without figures, and the pages of contemporary Sears, Roebuck catalogues were filled with bronze sculptures that could be purchased separately for placement on "plain parlor mantel clocks."

Almost all the clock manufacturers of the period contributed to this popular form, chief among them Ansonia, Gilbert, New Haven, Seth Thomas, and Waterbury. Most offered, as well, sentimental "novelty" figures (winsome milkmaids, cherubic little girls, and mischievous cupids, among others.) These should be contrasted with the figured mantel clocks of Florence Kroeber, highly prized by collectors today and justly so.

42-O Figured Mantel Clock (color plate)
"Figurine"
Florence Kroeber
New York, NY, c. 1890
H. 17", W. 16", D. 5½"

Victorian period, classical and Chippendale influences, cast-iron case and figure gilded and painted black; 8-day brass spring-driven movement; white enameled dial, slow-fast mechanism, Roman chapters, time and strike. On dial "F. K." **(F)**

NAWCCM, Inc.

42-1 Figured Mantel Clock
Maker unknown
Paris, France, for American
market, c. 1800
H. 21", W. 8½", D. 5½"

Federal period, Roman influence, brass case and bust of Washington, American eagle on plinth below clock, brass bun feet, brass dial, Roman chapters, time and strike. **(A)**

Israel Sack, Inc., N.Y.C.

42-2 Figured Mantel Clock
Dubuc
Paris, France, for American
market, c. 1810
H. 19½", W. 14", D. 5½"

Federal period, Roman influence, fire-gilded brass case with figure of Washington, eagle atop globe, Roman and American patriotic emblems on all sides of case and base; Roman chapters, time and strike. On dial "Dubuc Rue Michel Le Compte № 33. Paris." Under eagle "E. Pluribus Unum." On case "Washington. First in War, First in Peace, First in the Hearts of his Countrymen." **(A)**

Israel Sack, Inc., N.Y.C.

42-3 Figured Mantel Clock
"Crystal Palace No. 1 Extra"
Waterbury Clock Company
Waterbury, CT, c. 1875
H. 17", W. 15", D. 7½"

Victorian period, Roman influence, glass dome, wood pedestal, brass bezel, mirror behind pendulum reflects movement, iron figures; 8-day spring-driven movement, simulated mercury-compensated vials; white paper on iron dial, time and strike. [Listed in 1875 catalogue for $9.50 to $20.25. Clock named for famous New York exhibition hall.] **(F)**

NAWCCM, Inc.

42-4 Figured Mantel Clock "Shakespeare"
Ansonia Clock Company
New York, NY, c. 1882
H. 15¼", W. 16½", D. 5¾"

Victorian period, classical and Chippendale influences, metal and gilt case, egg-and-dart molding across top of base, gilt lion's paw feet and scrolled center motif, figure of Shakespeare with quill and paper in hand, manuscript marked "Macbeth" next to sword, trumpet-shaped pendants hang from sides of dial case, wisdom lamp finial above dial; outside escapement; white enameled dial, Roman chapters, time and strike. **(F)**

William Penn Memorial Museum, Pennsylvania Historical and Museum Commission

42-5 Figured Mantel Clock "Elizabethan Mandolin Player"
Ansonia Clock Company
New York, NY, c. 1882
H. 17", W. 20", D. 7½"

Victorian period, French influence, metal, gilt and black base with gilt metal figure and movement case, egg and dart molding around dial; spring movement with outside escapement; white enameled dial, Arabic chapters, time and strike. **(F)**

42-6 Figured Mantel Timepiece "Knight"
New Haven Clock Company
New Haven, CT, c. 1890
H. 11", W. 11½", D. 3¼"

Victorian period, bronzed metal figure of a seated knight next to round brass clock case with brass chain hanging below; brass movement; white painted dial, Arabic chapters, spade hands, time only. On dial "Made by the New Haven Clock Co. New Haven, Conn. U.S.A." **(F)**

NAWCCM, Inc.

**42-7 Figured Mantel Clock
"Don Caesar and Don Juan"
Ansonia Clock Company
New York, NY, c. 1895
H. 21½", W. 26", D. 9½"**

Victorian period, metal case with center clock and two side figures of cavaliers, swords drawn, metal lion's paw feet, brass bezel, egg and dart molding; Brocot jeweled visible movement; white porcelain or enameled dial, Roman chapters, spade hands, slow-fast mechanism, time and strike. On dial "Manufactured by/The Ansonia Clock Company, New York, United States of America" and trademark. **(E)**

NAWCCM, Inc.

**42-8 Figured Mantel Clock
"Artist"
Ansonia Clock Company
New York, NY, c. 1900
H. 11", W. 14", D. 5"**

Victorian period, bronzed metal case with figure seated next to asymmetrically scrolled clock case, egg and dart brass molding around dial; brass movement; white porcelain dial, Arabic chapters, time and strike. On dial "Manfd. by Ansonia Clock Co. New York, U.S.A." [Listed in 1914 catalogue in a Japanese bronze finish, $18.00; in real bronze finish, $19.80.] **(F)**

NAWCCM, Inc.

43 | Mantel Clock Variations

Although many collectors are fond of speaking of "mantel clocks," the term is of limited use in categorizing timekeepers, since virtually any shelf clock could be (and was, in fact) displayed to advantage on a fireplace mantel. Even small timepieces, normally thought of as "boudoir" furnishings—delicate porcelain clocks and French-

inspired carriage timepieces, for example—had their place on bedroom mantels as frequently as on dressing tables. Nonetheless, the term "mantel clock" conjures up an image of a solid ornamental case meant as much for display as for practicality in the Victorian parlor, and it is this stolidly "middle-class" clock to which the term best applies.

While it is easy to classify such clocks into separate groups of their own—steeples, iron-fronts, blacks, parlor walnuts, and so on—the multiplicity of design over the years defies strict classification in many, many instances. In this section, therefore, the wide variety of mantel clock variations can be barely suggested. Among these variations, the camel-back and tambour styles (with characteristic sloping sides) were particularly popular during the first four decades of the present century. Mantel variations were frequently made from unusual materials and occasionally boasted cases made of copper, brass, crystal, or cloisonné. Among the most interesting of the clocks illustrated in this section is one made of painted tiles that anticipates the asymmetrical Art Nouveau style by several years (see color plate 43).

43-O Mantel Clock Variation (color plate)
John G. Low, maker
Arthur Osborne, probable tile painter
Chelsea, MA, c. 1885
H. 12½", W. 9⅞", D. 5⅞"

Victorian period, English and Oriental influences, bronze case with purple glazed-tile panels, wave and Chinese key patterns ornament base and case; vine, leaf, and insect designs suggest asymmetry of French Art Nouveau; white porcelain dial, Arabic chapters, time and strike. Impressed on tiles "J. & J. G. Low/Patent/Art Tile Works,/Chelsea,/ Mass., U.S.A./Copyright 1884 by J. G. & J. F. Low." Ink stamped on tiles "Pat. applied for/Copyright 1885 by J. G. & J. F. Low."

Marco Polo Stufano

43-1 Mantel Clock Variation
"Oriental"
E. Ingraham & Company
Bristol, CT, c. 1861
H. 18"

Victorian period, Oriental influence, very round Gothic wood case ending in severe point on top and in two turnip-shaped supports above base, one volute between the supports; 8-day spring movement; white dial, Roman chapters, time and strike. **(D)**

43-2 Mantel Clock Variation
"Sonora Chimes"
Thomaston, CT, c. 1900
H. 13¾", W. 15", D. 7"

Victorian period, stained rose-wood case, brass bezel; 8-day brass spring-driven movement, Westminster chimes; white enameled dial, Arabic chapters, slow-fast mechanism, spade hands, time and strike. On dial "Seth Thomas/S & F/Sonora Chimes" **(F)**

NAWCCM, Inc.

43-3 Mantel Clock Variation
"Tambour"
Thomaston, CT, c. 1900
H. 9½", W. 19½", D. 5½"

Victorian period, pine and rosewood veneer case; brass movement; silvered dial, Arabic chapters, slow-fast mechanism, time and strike. On dial "Seth Thomas/Made in U.S.A." **(G)**

NAWCCM, Inc.

43-4 Mantel Clock Variation
"Bronze Mantel Clock"
Tiffany & Company, manufacturer
Chelsea Clock Company, movement
New York, NY and Boston, MA, c. 1900
H. 15¾", W. 12"

Victorian period, classical and Empire influences, bronze case with free-standing Doric columns and stylized bracket feet; silvered metal dial, Arabic chapters, slow-fast mechanism, time and strike. **(D)**

Sotheby Parke Bernet

43-5 Mantel Timepiece Variation
"Cloisonne Table Timepiece"
Probably New Haven Clock Co.
New Haven, CT, c. 1900
H. 8", W. 4"

Victorian period, Near Eastern influence, vitreous glaze poured into cloisons (compartments) and fused to metal surface, thin stand, rectangular base, gilded paw feet; 8-day movement; white porcelain dial, Arabic chapters, time only. On dial "New Haven, U.S.A." **(F)**

Lorretta Marder Interiors

43-6 Mantel Clock Variation
"Camel Back"
Sessions Clock Company
Forestville, CT, c. 1910
H. 12", W. 17"

Modern period, oak case; 8-day movement; white porcelain dial, time and strike. On dial "Sessions Clock Co.—Forestville, Conn., U.S.A." **(G)**

Lorretta Marder Interiors

43-7 Mantel Clock Variation
E. A. Brown Company, manufacturer
Chelsea Clock Company, movement
St. Paul, MN and Boston, MA, c. 1910
H. 16", W. 16"

Modern period, fruitwood case; 8-day movement; silver chapter ring, black raised, Arabic chapters, gold fretwork center, time and strike. Inscribed on movement "Chelsea Clock Co., Boston." Painted on dial "E. A. Brown Co., St. Paul." **(G)**

Lorretta Marder Interiors

43-8 Mantel Clock Variation
"Admiral"
Tiffany & Company, manufacturer
Chelsea Clock Company, movement
New York, NY and Boston, MA, c. 1910
H. 14¼", W. 13", D. 6¾", Diam. 8"

Modern period, red brass case on mahogany base; jeweled movement; engraved silvered dial, Arabic chapters, time, strike in nautical hours. On dial "Tiffany & Co., New York." "Pat'd Oct. 25, 1898; Sept. 19, 1890; June 5, 1900; also Patented Great Britain May 31, 1900." [This is the largest of Chelsea's ship's clocks.] **(E)**

W. G. Harding

43-9 Mantel Clock Variation
"Tambour"
Maker unknown
Probably CT, c. 1915
H. 9½", W. 20", D. 4"

Modern period, oak case, brass bezel; 8-day metal movement; white painted paper on tin painted dial, Roman chapters, diamond-shaped hands, time and strike. **(G)**

Private Collection

43-10 Mantel Clock Variation
Seth Thomas Clock Company
Thomaston, CT, c. 1915
H. 16⅞", W. 5¾", D. 9½"

Modern period, imitation rosewood veneer case made of celluloid, stylized arched top; 8-day movement; white dial, Arabic chapters, time and strike. On dial and on movement appears the name Seth Thomas. **(G)**

W. G. Harding

**43-11 Mantel Clock Variation
"Ship's Wheel Dial"
Waterbury Clock Company
Waterbury, CT, c. 1930
H. 10 ", W. 18 ", D. 3¾ "**

Modern period, brass case and wheel on oak platform, four bun feet; nautical 8-bell half-hour striking; silvered dial, Arabic chapters, time and strike. On dial "Waterbury/Jeweled Movement/ Made in USA by Waterbury Clock Co." **(G)**

NAWCCM, Inc.

---

44 | Cabinet (Gingerbread) Clocks

The most common—and, until recently, scorned—prototypes of the high-Victorian style are the "gingerbread"-decorated house and the "gingerbread"-decorated clock. The first gingerbread cabinet timekeepers were advertised by their makers simply as "walnut mantel clocks" or "visible pendulum spring clocks." Today they are perhaps best classified as "parlor walnuts," a term reflecting their formal purpose in the homes of the Victorian middle classes. The fundamental style of these clocks is Renaissance Revival or Baroque Revival, both exceptionally popular furniture styles in the final third of the nineteenth century.

Reaching their height of popularity in the 1880s, although the style remained in vogue until at least the turn of the century, parlor walnuts were joined by another gingerbread cabinet form, a less formal type of clock now known as "kitchen oaks." With new woods—walnut and oak—replacing the rosewood and mahogany popular in the Empire period, and an incised, flat, vaguely oriental design replacing the taste for carved, turned design, kitchen oaks reflect in every way the Victorian triumph of the machine. Circular saws and press-molding equipment suggest that the cases of these clocks were literally stamped out by the tens of thousands. Although kitchen oaks are now highly collectible (as well as easily accessible and affordable), their eclectic style, incorporating unrelated and even incompatible ornamentation, remains difficult to fathom uncritically. It is not uncommon, for example, to find a single kitchen oak with classical dart-and-egg molding, Eastlake cabinetry, and Egyptian palm tree designs.

Cabinet clocks—both parlor walnuts and kitchen oaks—were made in great number by all the major American clock manufacturers. Like many styles of late-Victorian mantel clocks, "gingerbread" clocks were frequently equipped with striking mechanisms for hours and cathedral gongs to strike the half hour.

44-0 Cabinet Clocks
"Topaz," "Kitchen Oak" (color plate, left)
E. Ingraham Company
Bristol, CT, c. 1880
H. 23", W. 14", D. 4", Dial 6"

Victorian period, Baroque and Rococo influences, press-molded oak case, egg and dart molding around door, gilded flowering tree and geometric designs on glass panel; 8-day calendar movement with barometer and thermometer; white painted metal dial, Roman chapters, outer calendar dial with Arabic numerals, time and strike. On back "The E. Ingraham Co. Bristol, Ct. U.S.A." **(F)**

"Patti," "Parlor Walnut" (color plate, right)
E. N. Welch Manufacturing Company
Bristol, CT, c. 1885
H. 19", W. 10½", D. 5"

Victorian period, Baroque and Rococo influences, walnut case, wooden ball finials, gilded geometric border on glass tablet, green Greek cross on pendulum bob; 8-day brass "Patti" movement, floating mainspring barrel, dead-beat escapement, solid pinions; white painted metal dial, Roman chapters, time and strike (cathedral gong). [The clock (and its movement) were named for opera star Adelina Patti. The patent covered case design and movement.] **(F)**

NAWCCM, Inc.

44-1 Cabinet Clock
"Parlor Walnut"
E. N. Welch Manufacturing Company
Bristol, CT, c. 1880
H. 23⅞", W. 14½", D. 5⅛"

Victorian period, walnut case, gold stenciled design with three knights in armor, (two of them mounted on horses); 8-day movement; white dial, brass alarm ring exposed, Roman chapters, time, strike, and alarm. Movement and label bear the name of E. N. Welch. **(F)**

W. G. Harding

44-2 Cabinet Clock
"Parlor Walnut"
Welch, Spring & Company
Bristol, CT, c. 1880
H. 19", W. 12½", Dial 6¼"

Victorian period, Baroque influence, walnut case with turned gallery-like fretwork across top, single finial, half-round turned engaged columns, molded base; 8-day movement; white painted dial, Roman chapters, separate brass alarm ring in center, time, strike, and alarm. **(F)**

44-3 Cabinet Clock
"Parlor Walnut"
New York, NY, c. 1880
H. 16", W. 9", D. 7½"

Victorian period, solid walnut case with brass trim, five brass finials, engaged wood and scrolled brass columns, molded wood base, brass flat-bun feet; 8-day spring movement; white painted dial, Roman chapters, time and strike. **(F)**

44-4 Cabinet Clock
"Kitchen Oak"
New Haven Clock Company
New Haven, CT, c. 1882
H. 20¾", W. 13½", D. 5"

Victorian period, Oriental influence, press-molded case with wood balls as finials, wheat and flowers painted on glass, simulated reeded pilasters, arched top; 8-day brass spring-driven movement, simple regulating device on bob; white painted dial, Roman chapters, spade hands, time and strike. On pendulum bob "S-F/Pat-d. Mch. 1st 1881" **(F)**

NAWCCM, Inc.

44-5 Cabinet Clock
"Patti," "Parlor Walnut"
E. N. Welch Manufacturing
Company
Forestville, CT, c. 1887
H. 19 ", W. 12¼ ", D. 6⅛ "

Victorian period, Baroque influence, walnut case, architectural-arch top with ball and ring-type machine-turned finials; engaged ring-type machine-turned columns with volute forms at top, center, and bottom of columns; gilt border on glass tablet; brass movement; white dial, Roman chapters, time and strike. On label "Eight Day/PATTI/Manufactured by/E. N. Welch Mfg. Co./ Forestville, Conn. U.S.A." [Another version of 44-0, but with bell strike.] **(F)**

NAWCCM, Inc.

44-6 Cabinet Clock
"Khedive," "Parlor Walnut"
E. N. Welch Manufacturing
Company
Forestville, CT, c. 1890
H. 18 ", W. 11¾ ", D. 6½ "

Victorian period, Baroque influence, walnut case, architectural molded cornice, free-standing wood columns, gilt border on lower rectangular tablet, brass bezel, brass egg and dart design around dial; "Patti" movement with visible jeweled Brocot deadbeat escapement and "floating" mainspring barrels; white painted dial, Roman chapters, fast-slow mechanism, time and strike. On back plate is stamped E. N. Welch Manufacturing Company. **(F)**

NAWCCM, Inc.

44-7 Cabinet Clock
"Kitchen Oak"
E. Ingraham & Company
Bristol, CT, c. 1894
H. 23 "

Victorian period, Oriental influence, oak case on raised molded base with stylized pilasters and arched top, gilded scroll design on glass tablet; 8-day movement, metal pendulum bob; white painted dial, Roman chapters for time, Arabic numerals in outer ring for date, separate date hand, time and strike with cathedral gong. **(F)**

44-8 Cabinet Clock
"No. 15," "Kitchen Oak"
E. Ingraham & Co., manufacturer
Bristol, CT, c. 1895
H. 15½ ", W. 14 ", D. 5½ "

Victorian period, press-molded oak case, anthemion leaf designs pressed on sides, rectangular clear-glass pendulum bob opening, pressed sheet-metal ornament in center, brass bezel; 8-day brass movement; white paper dial, Arabic chapters, time and strike; hours are struck on cathedral gong and half-hours on cup bell. Listed in 1904 catalogue for $4.75. **(F)**

NAWCCM, Inc.

44-9 Cabinet Clock
"Kitchen Oak"
Seth Thomas Clock Company
Thomaston, CT, c. 1895
H. 15¾ ", W. 11½ ", D. 5¾ "

Victorian period, Oriental influence, press-molded oak case, engaged, split spindle columns, pressed fretwork-type top, single finial, raised wood platform, egg and dart brass molding, brass bezel; brass movement; white paper dial, Roman chapters, spade hands, time and strike. On dial "S T"/"U.S.A." **(F)**

NAWCCM, Inc.

44-10 Cabinet Clock
"Kitchen Oak"
E. Ingraham & Company
Bristol, CT, c. 1895
H. 22 ", W. 13½ ", D. 4½ "

Victorian period, Oriental influence, press-molded oak case with Gothic top and evergreen-tree finials, gilded geometric design on glass tablet, simulated reeded pilasters; brass movement; white dial, Roman chapters, spade hands, time and strike. **(F)**

NAWCCM, Inc.

44-11 Cabinet Clock
"Sapphire," "Kitchen Oak"
The E. Ingraham Company
Bristol, CT, c. 1904
H. 22", W. 14"

Modern period, Renaissance, Eastlake and Oriental influences, press-molded oak case, glass tablet painted in geometric and palm designs; white enameled metal dial, Roman chapters, time, strike, and alarm. On label "SAP-PHIRE/Manufactured By/The E. Ingraham Company, Bristol, Conn., U.S.A." **(F)**

William Penn Museum, Pennsylvania Historical and Museum Commission

44-12 Cabinet Clock
"Parlor Walnut"
William Gilbert Clock Company
Winsted, CT, c. 1904
H. 22", W. 13", D. 3"

Modern period, Renaissance influence, walnut case with Baroque split spindle placed across base, stylized shaped columns on plinths, architectural top with stylized wooden finial above arch; white painted dial, Roman chapters, time and strike. **(F)**

Mr. & Mrs. Charles H. Gale

44-13 Cabinet Clock
"Parlor Walnut"
Sessions Clock Company
Forestville, CT, c. 1904
H. 23$_0$, W. 14$_0$, D. 4$_0$

Modern period, Renaissance influence, walnut case, three knights in armor (two of them on horseback) etched on glass tablet, machine-made incised fretwork carving; white painted dial, Roman chapters, time and strike. [Except for the bottom base line, which here is straight, and the closed center of the dial, this clock is identical to one by E. N. Welch, (see 44-1) whose company was purchased by William E. Session in 1903.] Stamped on movement "Sessions Clock Co./Forestville, Conn." **(F)**

Mr. & Mrs. Charles H. Gale

44-14 Cabinet Timepiece
"Cosey Corner Q." "Adirondacks Type"
William L. Gilbert Clock Company
Winsted, CT, c. 1910
H. 14 ", W. 12 ", D. 4½ "

Modern period, Oriental influence, pressed oak wood with dog and deer hunt scene around dial; 30-hour spring-driven movement; brass over paper dial, Arabic chapters, slow-fast mechanism, time only. On dial "Gilbert" **(F)**

NAWCCM, Inc.

45 | Blacks

Marble has always been a celebratory material, and the use of marble in clocks has been no exception. Napoleon enjoyed the Roman-style marble clock cases with Egyptian ormolu mounts used in

France in his day and before him by Louis XVI and after him by Charles X. Napolean's victory in Egypt, and his incorporation of Egyptian culture into his own, influenced early-nineteenth-century American clock casemakers who looked to France for leadership in the arts. Napoleonic taste was revived at the end of the century. By 1870 Americans were designing small black-and-gilt plinths for use in effective and inexpensive shelf clock cases. Although Roman, Egyptian, and French revivals were by then no longer unusual in the world of the decorative arts, the cost and materials for the "antique" and "Egyptian" look had changed immensely with the new technology. Innovation and perhaps considerable compromise were part of the new horological product referred to today as "blacks."

Victorian American "marble" clocks were not often made from real marble. They were usually a painted paper on wood or iron and were described as having an "adamantine" or rigid finish. The Terry Clock Company catalogue of 1885, for example, refers to them as "enameled iron clocks." Also simulated were the "brass" mounts made of painted white metal, iron, or wood. Lion's-paw feet, side handles, and Corinthian rather than plain Doric or Ionic columns adorned the rectangular, black platform-shaped boxes. One variation made in St. Louis, Missouri, in 1900 contained a coin slot for a $2.50 gold piece. For obvious reasons it was called a "slot machine" clock.

Although Ansonia, Seth Thomas, and the William Gilbert companies joined others in producing large quantities of marbleized blacks, these clocks were until recent years consigned to junk shops as emblems of the "bad taste" of our grandparents. Now that the Victorian period is once again of interest to scholars and collectors, the humble "blacks" are ripe for revaluation, and rightly so. For forty years they ruled supreme as the clocks of the average American.

45-O Marbleized Black Clock (color plate)
"Boston Extra"
Ansonia Clock Company
New York, NY, c. 1914
H. 11", W. 15", Dial 4"

Modern period, classical and Empire influences, black enameled iron case, black columns with gilded Corinthian capitals and bases, gabled top, brass bezel, egg and dart molding around dial; 8-day spring-driven movement, jeweled Brocot visible escapement, white enameled metal dial, slow-fast mechanism, Roman chapters, time and strike (hour and half-hour gong). On dial Ansonia trademark. **(F)**

NAWCCM, Inc.

45-1 Black Clock
"Curfew"
William L. Gilbert Clock Company
Winchester, CT, c. 1880
H. 18 ", W. 17 ", D. 6 "

Victorian period, Roman and Egyptian influences, wood case, gilt metal bell and arch, scrolled feet, bezel incised decoration; 8-day brass spring movement; Arabic chapters, time and strike. **(F)**

NAWCCM, Inc.

45-2 Black Clock
"The Alhambra"
Ansonia Clock Company
New York, NY, c. 1880
H. 19 ", W. 17 "

Victorian period, black lacquer wood case, original oil-painted panels with scenes and flowers, bronze ormulu strips; 8-day movement; porcelain visible escapement dial, time and strike. Printed on dial "Ansonia Clock Co., Patented." Label on back of clock "The Alhambra." **(F)**

Lorretta Marder Interiors

45-3 Black Clock
"Egypt Model"
Ansonia Clock Company
Brooklyn, NY, c. 1886
H. 10½ ", W. 16 ", D, 6½ "

Victorian period, Roman and Egyptian influences, iron case and pewter trim incised, gilt scroll design, brass bezel; 8-day movement; black rubberoid dial, Arabic chapters, time and strike. [Listed in 1886-87 catalogue for $23.50.] **(F)**

NAWCCM, Inc.

45-4 Black Clock
Maker unknown
Probably U.S.A., c. 1890
H. 8½", W. 13½", D. 6¼"

Victorian period, Roman and Egyptian influences, black marble incised gilt and green design; jeweled visible escapement wheel by Brocot; white porcelain dial, moon-type hands, Roman chapters, time and strike. **(F)**

NAWCCM, Inc.

45-5 Black Clock
"Unique"
Ansonia Clock Company
New York, NY, c. 1890
H. 10", W. 9¼", D. 4½"

Victorian period, Empire influence, flat cornice top, black-enameled iron case with incised decoration, brass bezel, egg and dart molding around dial; 8-day movement; white paper dial, Roman chapters, slow-fast mechanism, time and strike. On dial, Ansonia trademark and "Manufactured by the Ansonia Clock Co. New York United States of America." **(F)**

The Main Street Press

45-6 Marble Clock
Maker unknown
Probably CT, c. 1890
H. 13", W. 16", Dial 5½"

Victorian period, classical and Empire influences, white marble and metal case, two pairs of fluted black columns with Corinthian capitals and a Grecian female figure imposed between each pair, raised architectural form above dial, flaming torch motif in center; white dial, Arabic chapters, time and strike. **(F)**

B. C. & R. Roan, Inc.

45-7 Black Clock
"Java"
Waterbury Clock Company
Waterbury, CT, c. 1897
H. 11¼ ", W. 18¼ ", Dial 5½ "

Victorian period, Empire influence, wood case in imitation of black onyx, six marbleized columns with Corinthian capitals and brass bases; bronzed ram's head ornaments on side, scrolled brass feet, brass egg and dart molding around dial; 8-day movement; white dials, Roman chapters, time and strikes hour and half hours on cathedral gong bell. [Listed in Sears, Roebuck & Company 1897 catalogue for $6.30.] **(F)**

45-8 Black Clock
Seth Thomas Clock Company
Thomaston, CT, c. 1900
H. 11 ", W. 16½ ", D. 6¾ "

Victorian period, Roman and Egyptian influences, adamantine finish on pressed copper sheet on wood, engaged columns with marbleized bases, lion's-head side brackets, sheet-brass feet, brass-type bezel; 8-day movement; paper dial, cast sheet-brass pineapple ornament in center, Roman chapters, time, strike, and alarm. On dial "Manufactured in the United States of America." **(F)**

NAWCCM, Inc.

45-9 Marbleized Black Clock
"Dorena"
Waterbury Clock Co.
Waterbury, CT, c. 1900
H. 11 ", W. 15½ ", D. 7 "

Victorian period, marbleized wood and adamantine finish on wood, marbleized celluloid columns, sheet brass bracket feet, brass bezel surrounded by egg and dart molding; 8-day movement; white paper and wrought-brass dial, Roman chapters, fleur-de-lis hands, fast-slow mechanism, time and strikes hour and half-hours on cathedral gong and brass bell. **(F)**

The Main Street Press

45-10 Black Clock
"Sussex"
Seth Thomas Clock Company
Thomaston, CT. c. 1904-10
H. 10¾", W. 11½", D. 7", Dial 5"

Modern period, Roman and Egyptian influences, green and tan marbleized wood top, slight incising, scrolled bronzed metal feet, brass bezel surrounded by egg and dart molding, brass center medallion; 8-day movement; Arabic chapters, time and strike. On dial "Made by Seth Thomas Clock Co. Thomaston, Conn., U.S.A." [Listed in 1904-5 catalogue for $4.50. Listed in 1909-10 catalogue for $7.50.] **(F)**

NAWCCM, Inc.

45-11 Marbleized Black Clock
Ansonia Clock Company
New York City or Brooklyn, NY, c. 1905
H. 10½", W. 18", D. 6½"

Modern period, classical and Egyptian influences, black wood case, gilt lion's head handles, scrolled acanthus leaf feet; flat leaf and flower motifs in spandrel corners, on side panels, and on front base; gilt bezel; 8-day spring-driven movement; white dial, egg-and-dart molded inner ring, Roman chapters, time and strike. **(F)**

Greenfield Village and Henry Ford Museum

45-12 Black Clock
"Prince Elias"
Waterbury Clock Company
Waterbury, CT, c. 1908
H. 18½", W. 14", Dial 5"

Modern period, Roman influence, pediment top side columns with capitals and bases in wood enameled to imitate black marble, gilt feet, gilt scroll metal work on pediment base and sides, egg and dart molding in metal work around dial; 8-day spring movement; white paper and wrought-brass dial, Arabic chapters, fleur-de-lis hands, time and strikes hours and half hours on cathedral gong and brass bell. [Listed in 1908 Sears, Roebuck & Company catalogue for $3.62.] **(F)**

45-13 Marbleized Black Clock "Monarch"
New Haven Clock Company
New Haven, CT, c. 1910
H. 12 ", W. 17½ ", D. 6½ "

Modern period, classical and Egyptian influences, black wood case, four short marbleized Corinthian-style columns, four gilt mounts in spandrel corners, one large mount below dial; lion's paw feet; spring-driven movement; white dial, Arabic chapters, time and strike. On dial "Made by the New Haven Clock Co., New Haven, Conn., U.S.A." **(F)**

Greenfield Village and Henry Ford Museum

46 | Alarms

Simple "sound" alarms attached to mechanical timekeepers go back at least to 1534 when, under the rule of Henry VIII, an inventory of the Palace of Westminster listed a "clocke of Iron with a larum to the same with the Kinges Armes crownyd." Many hanging clocks, a few table clocks, and a number of tall-case clocks of the seventeenth and eighteenth centuries carried alarm components. Not all alarms, however, were as visible as the one designed for the typical nineteenth-century Connecticut pendulum shelf clock which featured a brass chapter ring attached to the outside center post of the dial.

A few quaint "action and sound" alarms are centuries old. The Germans, for example, introduced a table alarm in 1600 which was set to make a wheel lock produce sparks, which in turn ignited gunpowder, lit a candle, and woke the groggy sleeper, if not killed him in the process. In 1832 a Parisian invented a burning glass and a sun dial contraption to set off a cannon alarm. It must have awakened many deep sleepers. And in Victorian England, Lewis Carroll noted in his diaries an eccentric Oxford furniture dealer who invented an alarm clock which tipped its occupant out of bed at the time set for waking.

But today the timekeeper most commonly thought of as an alarm clock is the Big or Baby Ben variety, a three-to-five-inch round nickel-plated case standing on two small feet with an alarm bell and ring on the top. Alarms were advertised with calendar mechanisms in 1880 and with luminous dials making time visible in the dark by 1885. The animated alarm (46-0), with a lever escapement reaching through the dial to give rotary motion to a figure on the dial's surface, constitutes one of the sound-and-action collectibles in the marketplace today.

Although Westclox (né the Western Clock Manufacturing Company) was surely the prime producer of alarm clocks, there were many, many others made by such prominent firms as the Waterbury Clock Company (from 1877), Seth Thomas (from 1879), the Lux Clock Manufacturing Company in Waterbury, Connecticut, and the E. Ingraham Company in Bristol, Connecticut.

46-0 Alarm Timepiece (color plate)
"Washerwoman"
Waterbury Clock Company
Waterbury, CT, c. 1880
H. 6½"

Victorian period, nickel-plated drum-shaped case, ring handle, automated woman on dial scrubs clothes on stave wash board when clock runs; one-day spring pin-pallet lever escapement; paper dial, Roman chapters, time and alarm. On movement "Waterbury Clock Co. Patented." **(F)**

W. G. Harding

46-1 Alarm Timepieces
"Miniature Alarm" (left)
Waterbury Clock Company
Waterbury, CT, c. 1900
Dial 2"

Victorian period, "gold-plated" drum-shaped case, bell on top; one-day lever spring movement; white dial, separate second hand and dial, Roman chapters, spade hands, time and alarm. **(G)**

"Nickel Novelty" (right)
Ansonia Clock Company
New York, NY, c. 1885
Dial 2"

Victorian period, "gold-plated" drum-shaped case, bell on top with ring handle; one-day spring lever movement; white dial, Roman chapters, spade hands, separate moon-shaped second hand, time and alarm. **(G)**

W. G. Harding

46-2 Alarm Timepiece
Western Clock Manufacturing
Company
La Salle, IL, c. 1930
H. 5", W. 4½", D. 1½"

Modern period, square white painted-metal case, one-day lever spring movement; white paper dial; separate second hand and dial, Arabic chapters, time and alarm. On dial "Westclox." **(G)**

Private Collection

46-3 Alarm Timepiece
"Searchlight"
Darche Manufacturing
Company
Chicago, IL, c. 1910
H. 8¾", W. 8", D. 4½"

Modern period, horizontal copper case with two bells in front and small light dial on top; spring movement worked on batteries, white dial, Arabic chapters, spade hands; slow-fast mechanism, separate second hand and dial, time and alarm. On dial "Manufactured By/Darche Mfg. Co./Chicago, Ill." On back "Searchlight" (trade mark registered) Electric Alarm Clock/Pat. July 12th 1910." **(F)**

NAWCCM, Inc.

46-4 Alarm Timepieces
"8-Day Alarm" (left)
Sessions Clock Company
Bristol-Forestville, CT, c. 1910
H. 6½", W. 5½", D. 2¼"

Modern period, nickel-plated case on metal platform; 8-day spring movement; silvered dial, Arabic chapters, separate second hand and dial, diamond-shaped hands, slow-fast mechanism, time and alarm. On dial "Sessions/8 Day Alarm" and "Made in USA." **(G)**

"Liberator" (right)
E. Ingraham Company
Bristol, CT, c. 1910
H. 6¼", W. 6", D. 2¼"

Modern period, green crackled paint on metal case on similarly painted platform; spring movement; black dial, Arabic chapters, separate second hand and dial, time and alarm. On dial "Liberator/ Trade Mark Intermittent." On back, "Made by the E. Ingraham Co./ Bristol, Conn. U.S.A." **(G)**

NAWCCM, Inc.

46-5 Alarm Timepiece
"Flashlight, Alarm, and Bank"
Maker unknown
U.S.A., c. 1910
H. 8¼"

Modern period, metal novelty case, bell on front of case, deposit box also in front, brass bezel; spring movement; white dial, Arabic chapters, separate second hand and dial, time only. On clock: "Patented/ March 19, 1889;" "July 12, 1910" on casting. **(F)**

46-6 Alarm Timepiece
"Big Ben"
Western Clock Company
La Salle, IL, 1914
Dial 4½"

Modern period, nickel-plated case, two front feet, ring handle; lever movement; white dial, Arabic chapters, separate second hand and dial, time and alarm. Patented 1914. **(G)**

46-7 Alarm Timepieces
"National Call" (left)
E. Ingraham Clock Company
Bristol, CT, c. 1920
H. 6¼", W. 6", D. 2¼"

Modern period, round nickel-plated case on platform; spring movement, silent alarm, luminous black dial, Arabic chapters, slow-fast mechanism, time and alarm. On dial "National Call/8 Day Alarm, Luminous Dial and Hands, Reg. US Pat. Office." **(G)**

"Aurora" (right)
E. Ingraham Company
Bristol, CT, c. 1920
H. 7¼", W. 5½", D. 2¼"
Modern period, round nickel-plated case, two feet in front, handle on top; spring movement; Arabic chapters, slow-fast mechanism, separate second hand and dial, time and alarm. On dial "Aurora Trade Mark . . . Manufactured by The E. Ingraham Co., Bristol, Conn. U.S.A." **(G)**

NAWCCM, Inc.

46-8 Alarm Timepiece
"Knight" (left)
The Lux Clock Manufacturing Company
Waterbury, CT, c. 1922
H. 6¼", W. 4", D. 2¼"

Modern period, silvered case, bell on top with handle and two front feet; spring movement; white dial, Arabic chapters, separate second hand and dial, spade hands, time and alarm. On dial "Lux Knight . . . The Lux Clock Mfg. Co., Waterbury, Conn. U.S.A." On back "Patented/April 27, 1920,/Nov. 26, 1921/Made in U.S.A." **(G)**

"Sleep-Meter" (right)
Western Clock Company
La Salle, IL, c. 1920
H. 5½", W. 4", D. 2¾"

Modern period; silvered case, handle and feet; spring movement;
white dial, Arabic chapters, separate second hand and dial, time and
alarm. On dial "Westclox/Sleep-Meter/Made by Western Clock Co., La
Salle, Ill. U.S.A." On back "Patented/Dec. 5, 1908/Sept. 23, 1919/
Patents P.C.C." **(G)**

NAWCCM, Inc.

46-9 Alarm Timepieces
"Sleep-Meter" (left)
Western Clock Company
La Salle, IL, c. 1925
Dial 3¾"

Modern period, "gold-plated", drum-shaped case with two feet, ring
handle; one-day lever spring movement; white dial, Arabic chapters,
separate second hand and dial, time and alarm. **(G)**

"Ben-Hur" (center)
Western Clock Company
La Salle, IL, c. 1925
Dial 3¾"

Modern period, "gold-plated" drum-shaped case; one-day lever
spring movement; black dial, white Arabic chapters, separate second hand and dial, time and alarm. **(G)**

"Jack o'Lantern" (right)
Western Clock Company
La Salle, IL, c. 1925
Dial 3¾"

Modern period, "gold-plated", drum-shaped case with two feet, ring
handle; one-day lever movement; black dial, white Arabic chapters,
separate second hand and dial, time and alarm. **(G)**

W. G. Harding

**46-10 Alarm Timepiece
"Baby Ben"
Western Clock Manufacturing
   Company
La Salle, IL, c. 1926
Dial 2⅜"**

Modern period, "gold-plated" drum-shaped case with two feet, ring handle; one-day lever spring movement; black luminous dial, separate second hand and dial, white Arabic chapters, time and alarm. **(G)**

W. G. Harding

47 | Art Nouveau Clocks

By the last decade of the nineteenth century, American clockmakers, like American furniture designers, had responded to the effects of the simple line derived from Japanese art which entered the American design vocabulary in the 1860s, and to the use of natural materials coming out of the English Arts and Crafts movement of the 1860s and '70s. Also conscious of the soft, fluid, feminine spirit first called by a Parisian shopkeeper "Art Nouveau," American manufacturers included in their catalogues metal women and flowers that seemed to bend and flow like softening glass. Many of these clocks are essentially figured mantel clocks adapted to the Art Nouveau style.

Louis Comfort Tiffany was, of course, the great American designer of Art Nouveau glass lamps. His designs carried the French spirit to its highest American interpretative level. Although American Art Nouveau clocks rarely maintain the standard of Tiffany glass, the work by the New Haven, William Gilbert, and Ansonia clock manufactories represented the popular aesthetic mood of the nation prior to the stark and solid modernistic which followed in the early 1920s.

47-0 Art Nouveau Timepiece (color plate)
**New Haven Clock Company
New Haven, CT, c. 1900
H. 11", W. 6"**

Victorian period, gilded metal case with two female figures one on each side of case, profiled female in center in relief, porcelain dial, Arabic chapters, time only. Printed on dial: "Made by New Haven Clock Co., U.S.A." **(F)**

Lorretta Marder Interiors

**47-1 Art Nouveau Clock
New Haven Clock Company
New Haven, CT, c. 1895
H. 15", W. 7", D. 4"**

Victorian period, French Rococo influence, brass case with porcelain finial, musician and lady painted on porcelain tablet; white, enameled dial with floral ring, Arabic chapters, time and strike. On dial "New Haven U.S.A." **(F)**

Private Collection

**47-2 Art Nouveau Clock
Ansonia Clock Company
New York, NY, c. 1895
H. 16", W. 8"**

Victorian period, French influence, Louis V style, gilded metal with Royal Bonn porcelain inset of two angels; 8-day movement; porcelain dial, Roman chapters, time and strike. Inscribed on movement "Ansonia Clock Co., U.S.A." **(F)**

Lorretta Marder Interiors

**47-3 Art Nouveau Timepiece
New Haven Clock Company
New Haven, CT, c. 1895
H. 7"**

Victorian period, French influence, asymmetrically-shaped gilded metal case with rose as finial, leaves following curve of drum-shaped timepiece down to the four feet; brass movement; white dial, Arabic chapters, separate second hand and dial, time only. **(F)**

**47-4 Art Nouveau Clock
Ansonia Clock Company
New York, NY, c. 1900
H. 14", W. 9"**

Victorian period, French influence, gilded metal case; 8-day movement; porcelain dial, Roman chapters, time and strike. Printed on dial "Mfd. by the Ansonia Clock Company, New York, U.S.A." **(F)**

Lorretta Marder Interiors

47-5 Art Nouveau Clock "Alva"
William L. Gilbert Clock Company
Winsted, CT, c. 1900
H. 14½", W. 8½"

Victorian period, asymmetrical French Rococo influence, wood case covered with brown paper, gilded cast-metal trim, brass bezel; 30-hour movement; white, painted dial, Arabic chapters, time, strike, and alarm. **(F)**

Greenfield Village and Henry Ford Museum

47-6 Art Nouveau Timepieces
New Haven Clock Company (left)
New Haven, CT, c. 1895
H. 6", W. 4", D. 2"

Victorian period, French Rococo influence, rectangular gilded cast-iron carriage-type case, asymmetrically-designed floral decoration, handle; brass spring movement; white enameled dial, Arabic chapters, spade hands, time only. On dial "New Haven/U.S.A." and "Made by The New Haven Clock Co. New Haven, Conn. U.S.A." **(F)**

"No B2517" (right)
Jennings Bros. Mfg. Co.
Bridgeport, PA, c. 1906
H. 4½", W. 3½", D. 1½"

Victorian period, French Rococo influence, gilded cast-iron case, asymmetrically-designed with two roses (one on right and one on top), natural forms become the feet; one-day brass spring movement; porcelain dial, Arabic chapters, slow-fast mechanism, spade hands, separate second hand and dial, time only. On bottom "J.B." [Listed in 1906 catalogue for $2.00.] **(F)**

NAWCCM, Inc.

**47-7 Art Nouveau Clock
"Calais"
Ansonia Clock Company
New York, NY, c. 1914
H. 14", W. 7½", D. 2½"**

Modern period, French Rococo influence, cast-iron case with gilt and green spackled paint, applied brass ornament and asymmetrical finial, brass-scrolled feet; egg and dart molding around dial, brass ornament separating Arabic chapters on dial, time and strike (hour and half-hour). [Listed in 1914 catalogue for $7.75.] **(F)**

48 | Mission Oak Clocks

Like Art Nouveau, the Mission style was a response to the over-decorated and misused machine materials now referred to as "high Victorian." The theories of John Ruskin in the '50s and '60s, the philosophy of William Morris in the '70s, and the Arts and Crafts movement in the '80s and '90s induced furniture designers like Gustav Stickley to return to "nature," to objects which displayed their function, to the flat geometric form, to "honest" woods like oak, and to a fervent denial of the role of the machine in the twentieth century.

The name "Mission" is attributed by some to the functionalist designer's sense of having been driven by an inner, moral commitment or a mission to create designs which were simple and pure. Others claim that the term derived from the presence of oak in the sparse Franciscan missions of California. Clearly, the Mission oak clock, in figure-eight, schoolhouse, and tower shelf forms, bears the composition of a simple non-revivalist ideal and was made in the shadow of an impossible belief that there could be a human creator with an innocent eye.

48-O Mission Oak Timepiece (color plate)
**"Jupiter"
Sessions Clock Company
Forestville, CT, c. 1915
H. 17", W. 8¼", D. 4¼"**

Modern period, solid-oak weathered-finish case; 8-day movement; wooden dial, applied metal Arabic chapters, spade hands, time only. On label "Sessions Clock Co./Successor to the N. E. N. Welch Mfg. Co. Forestville, Conn. U.S.A./Eight Day Time" [Listed in 1915 catalogue for $3.70, with strike for $4.74.] **(F)**

NAWCCM, Inc.

48-1 Mission Oak Clock
New Haven Clock Company
New Haven, CT, c. 1910
H. 13¾", W. 11¾", D. 5½"

Modern period, black oak case with flat top, grillwork design below dial, stylized bracket feet; 8-day movement; black dial, applied metal Arabic chapters, time and strike. **(F)**

48-2 Mission Oak Clock
New Haven Clock Company
New Haven, CT, c. 1910
H. 21", W. 13¼", D. 4½"

Modern period, Arts and Crafts influence, black stained oak, splay-shaped case, bracket-type feet, shaped pediment top, sloped cut apron; 8-day spring-driven pendulum movement; applied brass Arabic chapters, time and strike. **(F)**
NAWCCM, Inc.

48-3 Mission Oak Clock
"Los Barrios"
New Haven Clock Company
New Haven, CT, c. 1910
H. 13½", W. 11¼", D. 4½"

Modern period, Arts and Crafts influence, dark-stained oak splayed-type case with open grillwork below dial; 8-day spring-driven pendulum movement; applied brass chapters and hands, time and strike (hour and half-hour on cathedral gong). [Listed originally for $4.90.] **(F)**
NAWCCM, Inc.

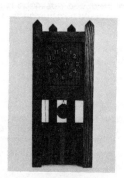

48-4 Mission Oak Timepiece
"Miniature Mission Alarm"
Sessions Clock Company
Bristol-Forestville, CT. c. 1910
H. 14½", W. 6¼", D. 3¾"

Modern period, Arts and Crafts influence, dark-stained oak tower-like case, brass alarm ring; 8-day brass spring-driven pendulum movement with separate alarm in base; wood dial, applied brass Arabic chapters, time and alarm. **(G)**
NAWCCM, Inc.

48-5 Mission Oak Timepiece
"Miniature Mission"
William L. Gilbert Clock
  Company
Winsted, CT, c. 1910
H. 14¾", W. 4½", D. 3½"

Modern period, Arts and Crafts influence, black stained oak tower-like case; applied metal Arabic chapters, time only. **(G)**

NAWCCM, Inc.

48-6 Mission Oak Timepiece
Parker Clock Company
Meriden, CT, c. 1915
H. 11½", W. 5½", D. 3⅝"

Modern period, Arts and Crafts influence, black-stained oak tower-like case; 30-hour spring-driven movement; white paper dial Roman chapters, separate second hand, time and alarm. On dial "Made by The Parker Clock Co. Meriden, Conn. U.S.A." and "Trademark Parker." **(G)**

NAWCCM, Inc.

48-7 Mission Oak Timepiece
"Lute"
New Haven Clock Company
New Haven, CT. c. 1910
H. 9", W. 4½", Dial 2"

Modern period, Arts and Crafts influence, dark-stained solid-oak cruciform case on oak base; one-day lever movement; blue painted dial in center of cross, applied white chapters, white hands, time only. [Listed originally for $2.80.] **(G)**

49 | Art Deco Clocks

Rising up out of a need to be truly of its own unmimetic time, to be anti-historical, to be unrooted, without a past, and unmindful of the possibility of having any future, the style now called Art Deco dominated the period between 1918 and 1939, although its impact in America began only slowly after 1925. Freed of a dependence upon traditional design, the Art Deco timepiece was a baby of the streamlined, flexible impulse, an innocent in the world of inherited images. Art Deco was taken on by potters, metal workers, architects, glass makers, furniture manufacturers, and the new world of synthetics producers. It frequently embodied the horizontal look rather than the vertical line of its predecessor Art Nouveau. It was rational, although some say that it was also hideous in its stark, low robustness.

Art Deco clocks were made from smooth-looking materials— Celluloid, Fiberloid, Bakelite, Durez, Makalot, Arcolite, and other man-made products. Synthetics conformed easily to the new design of round-cornered square clocks. Art Deco attempted to look functional and streamlined ("modern," in short) by affecting single, double, and triple chrome lines that moved horizontally across the clock case to emphasize planes and motion—the same message of modernity being read across buildings and locomotives of the period. Although American Art Deco clocks were designed by such masters as Gilbert Rohde (for the Herman Miller Company), the collector should be aware that most American Art Deco clocks are vastly inferior in design to their Continental counterparts.

49-O Art Deco Timepiece (color plate)
Tiffany & Company
New York, NY, c. 1930
7″ square

Modern period, boudoir clock, nickel-plated brass case with grey marble corner insets (stands on easel back); 8-day movement; silver dial, Arabic chapters, unusual "alligator" hands and chapters, time only. Painted on dial "Tiffany & Co." **(E)**

Lorretta Marder Interiors

49-1 Art Deco Timepieces
"Vanitie" (left)
Maker unknown
U.S.A., c. 1931
H. 4½″, W. 6¾″, D. 2½″

Modern period, black metal case with brass strips around square dial and across front of case; steel-spring lever escapement; white dial, Arabic chapters, time and alarm. On dial "Vanitie/Made in U.S.A." On back "Patented March 31, 1931/Made in U.S.A." **(G)**

"La Sallita" (right)
Western Clock Company
La Salle, IL, c. 1929
H. 3¼ ", W. 3½ " D. 1¼ "

Modern period, black plastic with chrome strip; 30-hour pull wind movement; chrome dial, Arabic chapters, time only. On back "La Sallita Patented U.S.A. 1563431, 1709146, 1848520" and "Made by Westclox La Salle, Ill., U.S.A." **(G)**

NAWCCM, Inc.

49-2 Art Deco Timepiece
Waltham Watch Company
Waltham, MA, c. 1930
H. 11¼ ", W. 10½ ", D. 3½ "

Modern period, walnut shield-shaped case on walnut base; 8-day double main-spring (#37 model) movement, 7 jewels; silvered dial, stylized metallic Arabic chapters, time only. On dial "Waltham." **(G)**

NAWCCM, Inc.

49-3 Art Deco Timepieces
"Octagonal Desk" (left)
Lux Clock Manufacturing Company
Waterbury, CT, c. 1930
H. 5½ ", W. 8 ", D. 2 "

Modern period, bronze octagonal case on shaped base; 30-hour steel spring lever escapement; bronzed dial, Arabic chapters, slow-fast mechanism, time only. On dial "Design Registered" and "The Lux Clock Mfg. Co., Waterbury, Conn. U.S.A." **(G)**

"Silvercraft" (right)
New Haven Clock Company
New Haven, CT, c. 1930
H. 5¼ ", W. 6¼ ", D. 2¼ "

Modern period, square silvered case and dial on green plastic platform with silvered posts, Arabic chapters, diamond-shaped hands, time only. On back "Silvercraft." **(G)**

NAWCCM, Inc.

49-4 Art Deco Timepieces
"Boudoir or Dresser Timepieces"
Maker unknown
U.S.A., c. 1930
H. 4", W. 8" (left); **H. 3", W. 5"** (right)

Modern period, celluloid case; 8-day movement; paper dial, Arabic chapters, separate second hand and dial, time only. Printed on dial "Made in U.S.A." **(G)**

Lorretta Marder Interiors

49-5 Art Deco
Gilbert Rohde, designer; Herman Miller
Furniture Company, manufacturer
Zeeland, MI, c. 1935
H. 6¼", W. 16¾", D. 3¼"

Modern period, rosewood and chrome case; white dial, separate second hand, stylized Arabic chapters. On dial "Herman Miller." **(F)**

The Metropolitan Museum of Art

50 | Shelf Novelties and Specialties

Once miniaturization and mass production of clocks were perfected in post-Civil War America, and even the most ordinary citizen was assured a reasonably accurate timekeeper for as little as a dollar, clockmakers turned their attention to variety and novelty, to satisfying a seemingly endless demand for the new, the inventive, the sentimental—all in keeping with prevailing middle-class American tastes. The matter, after all, was essentially simple: the same movement could be easily inserted in any variety of case, no matter how incongruous the result. And the result, to say the least, was frequently incongruous indeed. In one year alone (1891) the Ansonia Clock Company offered timepieces set within bronze locomotives, sailing ships, racing trotters, peacocks, Masonic insignias, padlocks, ladies' fans, horseshoes, wheelbarrows, inkwells, picture frames, and suits of armor, just to name a few cases. Little children, portrayed in a variety of sentimental poses, and cupids discreetly draped were turn-of-the-century favorites. In this vein, the Jennings Manufacturing Company featured a cupid climbing a miniature street clock, a crocodile snapping at the cuddly creature's exposed posterior. While they are great fun to examine and collect, these novelties demonstrate that the twentieth century hardly has a monopoly on inventiveness or bad taste.

Specialties, unlike novelties, are created to fill a special need. The first automobile timepieces, for example, bear little resemblance to the clocks in today's cars. Made to project from the dashboards of Tin Lizzies—an extension of the shelf if ever there was one—these timepieces are both aesthetically pleasing and highly collectible. The pages that follow can just hint at the great variety of novelties and specialties that were produced over the years.

50-O Novelty Timepiece (color plate)
"Bobbing Doll"
Ansonia Clock Company
New York, NY, c. 1887
H. 14½", W. 4", D. 6¼"

Victorian period, nickel-plated case, bisque doll; 30-hour timepiece, up and down motion of doll acts as pendulum; white dial, separate second hand and dial, Roman chapters, time only. On dial "Patented Dec. 14th/1886." **(E)**

W. G. Harding

50-1 Novelty Timepiece
"No. 5002 Candlestick"
Seth Thomas Clock Company
Plymouth Hollow, CT, c. 1863
H. 10" Including dome, Diam. 6"

Victorian period, black painted and gilt pedestal, glass dome; 8-day balance wheel movement, dead-beat escapement; white enameled dial, Roman chapters, spade hands, time only. **(F)**

NAWCCM, Inc.

50-2 Novelty Clock
"Illuminated Alarm"
Henry J. Davis, patentee
Ansonia Brass & Copper Company
Brooklyn, NY and Ansonia, CT, c. 1876
H. 16", W. 7¼", D. 3⅝"

Victorian period, mahogany and veneer box case, scrolled design painted on lower glass panel, case above dial holds cup for matches, metal extension for single match above wick on oil can hidden under top board; brass alarm movement; white painted dial, brass alarm ring exposed in center, Roman chapters, time, strike, and alarm.

The National Museum of History and Technology, Smithsonian Institution

50-3 Novelty Timepiece
"Briggs Rotary Model II"
John C. Briggs, patentee
E. N. Welch Manufacturing Company, maker
Bristol, CT, c. 1878
H. 7½", W. 5", D. 5"

Victorian period, Empire influence, glass dome over wood base, paw feet; brass spring movement; white painted dial, Roman chapters, spade hands, time only. **(F)**

NAWCCM, Inc.

50-4 Novelty Timepiece
"Flying Pendulum," "Ignatz"
New Haven Clock Company
New Haven, CT, c. 1885
H. 10", W. 6½", D. 2½"

Victorian period, wood and brass case, metal paw feet and metal side handles, flying apparatus also brass; white painted dial, Roman chapters, time only. On dial "Pat'd Oct. 9th 1883/Jerome

& Co." [Manufactured only between 1884 and 1885; four models were produced; the prices varied from $7.50 to $10.00.] **(F)**

NAWCCM, Inc.

50-5 Novelty Timepiece "Mace"
New Haven Clock Company
New Haven, CT, c. 1886
H. 4", W. 4", D. 4"

Victorian period, brass mace form with dial indicating it was a "give away" advertising timepiece; spring double-roller club-tooth escapement, cut and polished-steel pinions, straight lever, screw pillars; paper dial, magnifying lens covers dial, Arabic chapters, time only. On dial "Red Label." Listed originally (without advertising) for $5.75. **(F)**

NAWCCM, Inc.

50-6 Novelty Clock "The Bell"
New Haven Clock Company
New Haven, CT, c. 1890
H. 14", W. 13", D. 5½"

Victorian period, metal bell-shaped case with brass finish; 8-day brass spring movement; white painted metal dial, brass scrolls in center, Arabic chapters, time and strike (cathedral gong). Case advertisement, "Drink Belle of Bourbon." **(F)**

NAWCCM, Inc.

50-7 Novelty Clock "Violin"
Seth Thomas Company
Thomaston, CT, c. 1890
H. 29", W. 13½"

Victorian period, violin-shaped case, applied leaf carving, glass panel decorated with gilt musical trophies, footed base white painted dial, Roman chapters, time and strike. **(D)**

Sotheby Parke Bernet

50-8 Specialty Timepiece "Never-Wind"
Tiffany Never-Wind Clock Corporation
Buffalo, NY, c. 1904
H. 11", Dial 6½"

Modern period, metal case; one-year torsion movement, magnetic battery-powered pendulum; white dial, Arabic chapters, time only. On dial "Never-Wind/Tiffany Never-Wind Clock Corporation, Buffalo, N.Y., U.S.A., Pat. March 8, 1904." **(F)**

Greenfield Village and Henry Ford Museum

50-9 Novelty Timepiece "Plato"
Eugene L. Fitch, inventor
Ansonia Clock Company, maker
New York, NY, c. 1905
H. 6", W. 3", D. 2½"

Modern period, brass and glass case, plates or pages turn to show time, carriage-type handle; brass spring digital movement; time only. "Patented Dec. 16, 1902; Apr. 28, 1903; Apr. 7, 1903; July 7, 1903" (issued to inventor). [40,000 estimated to have been produced; reproductions were made in France and Germany.] **(F)**

NAWCCM, Inc.

50-10 Novelty Timepiece "Gloria Ball Swing"
Ansonia Clock Company
New York, NY, c. 1904
H. 28½", W. 7", D. 7"

Modern period, classical influence, lacquered bronze winged female figure with lyre in one hand, swinging movement in other; double pendulum, 8-day brass movement with recoil escapement, small pendulum within movement case regulated in reverse of normal timepiece (lower ball is raised to make it work slower); time only. [Sold in 1904 for $43.00.] **(D)**

NAWCCM, Inc.

50-11 Specialty Timepieces "Automobile Dashboard Timepieces" Waltham Watch Company Waltham, MA, c. 1910-15

(left) **Dial 3⅜ "**

Modern period, nickel-plated brass case; 8-day 7-jewel movement; black metal dial, Arabic chapters and luminous hands, time only. Model #L, Serial #20,987,283. Name on movement. **(G)**

(center) **Dial 2½ "**

Modern period, nickel-plated brass case; 8-day 7-jewel movement; silvered metal dial, Arabic chapters, separate second hand and dial, time and alarm. **(G)**

(right) **Dial 2¾ "**

Modern period, nickel-plated brass case; 8-day 7-jewel movement; black metal dial, Arabic chapters, and luminous hands, time only. On dial "Model K-1, Serial No. 20,982,605." Name on movement. **(G)**

W. G. Harding

50-12 Specialty Timepieces "Automobile Dashboard Timepieces" Waltham Watch Company Waltham, MA, c. 1915-20

(left) **Dial 3⅜ "**

Modern period, nickel-plated brass with leaded back; 8-day 7-jewel watch-type movement; black metal dial, Arabic chapters, luminous hands, time only. Model #K-3; Serial #23230097. On dial "Waltham." **(G)**

(right) **Dial 2¾ "**

Modern period, nickel-plated brass case with leaded back; 8-day 7-jewel watch-type movement; silvered metal dial, Arabic chapters, separate second hand and dial, time only. Model #K-11; Serial #21,380,328. On dial, "Waltham." **(G)**

W. G. Harding

50-13 Novelty Timepiece
"Homestead"
Lux Clock Company
Waterbury, CT, c. 1927
H. 6", W. 9½", D. 3"

Modern period, painted compressed wood pulp case; brass movement; white painted dial, Arabic chapters, time only. [Described in 1927 Sears catalogue as "a modern house with attached garage and tile roof. Does not alarm."] On dial "Homestead/Lux Co., Waterbury, Conn." On back stamped "The Deluxe Clock and Mfg. Co. Homestead patent applied for." **(G)**

NAWCCM, Inc.

50-14 Novelty Timepiece
"Monitor Top"
Warren Telechron Company,
    maker
Ashland, MA, c. 1930
H. 8¾", W. 5", D. 3¼"

Modern period, white enameled iron case in shape of General Electric "Monitor Top" refrigerator; M-1 electric synchronous movement; white painted metal dial, Arabic chapters, separate second hand, time only. On dial "Telechron/Warren Telechron Co. Ashland, Mass." [21,000 "refrigerators" were produced for General Electric.] **(G)**

NAWCCM, Inc.

50-15 Novelty Timepiece
"FDR—Man of the Hour"
United Electric Clock Company
Brooklyn, NY, c. 1933
H. 14″, W. 8¼″, D. 2½″

Modern period, bronzed case (FDR steering ship of state), cocktail lounge scene painted on dial (celebrating repeal of 18th Amendment); powered by electric motor; Arabic chapters, time only. On dial "Made in U.S.A. 1933/United Electric Clock Co., Brooklyn, N.Y." On case "FDR— Man of the Hour." **(F)**

NAWCCM, Inc.

50-16 Novelty Timepiece
"Tape Measure"
Lux Manufacturing Company
Waterbury, CT, c. 1935
Diam. 5″

Modern period, metal case on a round base with a single pointer attached to base, chapter ring goes around case horizontally; horizontal and circular dial, time only. On base "Made in U.S.A./ Pat. No. D-95, 184" **(G)**

NAWCCM, Inc.

Acknowledgments

A book incurs many pleasant debts to colleagues, family, friends, and critics, to other writers, other books, collectors, and dealers, to the staffs of museums, libraries, and the publishing house. The author would particularly like to thank Stacy Wood, Jr., Carter Harris, Robert Sack, and Dana Blackwell. Their courtesy and generosity, their critical judgment and expertise, have been part of the making of this guide. The book could not have been completed without the cheerful industry of Doris Dinger who typed the manuscript, without the editorial skill of Martin Greif, and without the encouragement of an interested, patient, and supportive husband.

For the extraordinary range of photographs the following institutions and companies are gratefully thanked: National Association of Watch and Clock Collectors Museum, Inc.; The William Penn Memorial Museum; The National Gallery of Art, Index of American Design; Smithsonian Institution; Winterthur Museum; Museum of History and Technology; Greenfield Village and Henry Ford Museum; Willard House and Clock Museum; Firestone Library, Princeton University; Shelburne Museum, Inc.; Essex Institute; Colonial Williamsburg; Old Sturbridge Village; American Clock and Watch Museum; Newport Historical Society; The Art Institute of Chicago; The Metropolitan Museum; Israel Sack, Inc.; Sotheby Parke Bernet, Inc.; Samuel T. Freeman, Inc.; Robert W. Skinner, Inc.; The E. Howard Clock Company; B. C. & R. Roan, Inc.; H. & R. Sandor, Inc.; Lorretta Marder Interiors; Richard Don Antiques; Jordan-Volpe Gallery; and the Philip H. Bradley Co.

The author wishes to thank the following friends for their assistance and advice: Charles F. Hummel, Samuel M. Freeman 2nd, Harold Sack, Albert Sack, John and Christiana Batdorf, Deborah Batdorf, Robert C. Keeman, James Cogswell, Richard and Celia Oliver, Christopher Bailey, Warner D. Bundens, William Stahl, Nancy Druckman, Margaret and George W. Scott, Jr., W. G. Harding, Rose Brandt, Charles H. Gale, Irvin G. Schorsch III, Bonnie D. Schorsch, Cathryn J. McElroy, Bruce Bazelon, George Wood, Ann Farnham, John Wright, Joan and Joseph H. Reese, Jr., Victor and Joan Johnson, Skip Chalfont, Robert Cheyne, Marco Polo Stufano, Lou Powers, Donna Baron, Lina Steele, Madeline Wordell, Norman Langmaid, Bruce Shoemaker, Edgar and Charlotte Sittig, Milo Naeve, Roger and Imogene Robinson, Amerst E. Huson, Carolina Stevens, Martin Eidelberg, Tom Bruhn, Marilyn Bordes, George Fistrovitch, Karol Schmiegel, Jo Lynn Reisinger, Linda H. Russo, Elaine P. Menchey, Benjamin Brock, Mary Gardner, Terence McGough, Donald J. Summar, Jean R. Butler, Arthur F. Newell, and Clyde F. Brown.

All of the clocks from the collection of the National Association of Watch and Clock Collectors Museum, Inc. (NAWCCM, Inc.) included in this book were photographed by J. Michael Kanouff. Additional photographic credits are as follows:

Israel Sack, Inc., N.Y.C. (1-1, 19-5, 31-4); George Fistrovich (1-4, 1-9, 1-12); Dana J. Blackwell (7-8, 8-0, 11-8, 14-4, 23-4, 24-3, 28-1, 28-3, 41-0, 41-3).

Selected Bibliography

Allix, Charles. *Carriage Clocks: Their History and Development.* England: Baron Publishing Co., 1974.

Bailey, Chris H. *Two Hundred Years of American Clocks & Watches.* Englewood Cliffs, New Jersey: Prentice-Hall, Inc., 1975.

_____ and Blackwell, Dana J. "Heman Clark and the 'Salem Bridge' Shelf Clocks." *Supplement to Bulletin of NAWCC, Inc.* 13 (1980).

Battison, Edwin A. and Kane, Patricia E. *The American Clock 1725-1865.* Greenwich, Connecticut: New York Graphic Society Limited, 1973.

Bruton, Eric. *Clocks and Watches 1400-1900.* New York: Frederick A. Praeger, 1967.

Butler, Joseph. *American Antiques 1800-1900.* New York: The Odyssey Press, 1965.

Carlisle, Lilian Baker. "New Biographical Findings on Curtis & Dunning Girandole Clockmakers." *The American Art Journal* X, 1 (May 1978).

Chandlee, Edward E. *Six Quaker Clockmakers.* Philadelphia: The Historical Society of Pennsylvania, 1943; reprinted by The New England Publishing Company, 1975.

Cipolla, Carlo M. *Clocks and Culture 1300-1700.* London: Collins, 1967.

Clutton, C., et al. *Britten's Old Clocks and Watches and Their Makers.* New York: E.P. Dutton, 1973.

Coatney, G. Robert and Scholtens, Robert G. "Georgia-Made Clocks." *Bulletin of the NAWCC, Inc.* XVII, No. 5, Whole Number 178 (October 1975).

de Carle, Donald. *Watch & Clock Encyclopedia.* London: N.A.B. Press, Ltd., 1950; reprinted by Bonanza Books, 1977.

de Magnin, Paul R. "'Steeples' American Sharp Gothic Clocks and Variations." *Bulletin of the NAWCC, Inc.* XII, No. 9, Whole Number 127 (April 1967).

Dworetsky, Lester and Dickstein, Robert. *Horology Americana.* New York: Horology Americana, Inc., 1972.

Eckhardt, George H. *Pennsylvania Clocks and Clockmakers.* New York: The Devin-Adair Company, 1955.

Fleming, John and Honour, Hugh. *Dictionary of the Decorative Arts.* New York: Harper & Row, 1977.

Fried, Fred and Mary. *America's Forgotten Folk Art.* New York: Pantheon Books, 1978.

Grimshaw, Thomas E. "Fusee Beehive Clock." *Bulletin of NAWCC, Inc.* XXII, No. 4, Whole Number 207 (August 1980).

Hoopes, Penrose R. *Connecticut Clockmakers of the Eighteenth Century.* New York: Dover Publications, Inc., 1974.

Husher, R. W. and Welch, W. W. *A Study of Simon Willard's Clocks.* Nahant, Massachusetts: Husher and Welch, 1980.

Hummel, Charles F. *With Hammer in Hand.* Charlottesville: The University Press of Virginia, 1968.

Jerome, Chauncey. *History of the American Clock Business.* New Haven, 1860.

Kochmann, Karl. *The Black Forest Cuckoo Clock.* Concord, California: Antique Clocks Publishing, 1978.

La Fond, E. F., Jr. "Frederick Heisley Strikes Again." *Bulletin of the NAWCC, Inc.* XIII, No. 3, Whole Number 133 (April 1968).

Lloyd, H. Alan. *Some Outstanding Clocks Over Seven Hundred Years 1250-1950.* London: Leonard Hill (Books) Limited, 1958.

Milham, Willis I. *Time & Timekeepers.* London: Macmillan and Co., Limited, 1923.

Palmer, Brooks. *The Book of American Clocks.* New York: The Macmillan Company, 1950.

_____. *A Treasury of American Clocks.* New York: The Macmillan Publishing Co., Inc., 1977.

Roberts, Kenneth D. *Eli Terry and the Connecticut Shelf Clock.* Bristol, Connecticut: Kenneth D. Roberts Publishing Company, 1973.

_____. *The Contributions of Joseph Ives to Connecticut Clock Technology 1810-1862.* Hartford, Connecticut: The Bond Press, Inc., 1970.

Roehrich, Mary. "'Regulator' Defined." *Bulletin of NAWCC, Inc.* XIII, No. 5, Whole Number 135 (August 1968).

Schwartz, Marvin D. *Collectors' Guide to Antique American Clocks.* New York: Doubleday & Company, Inc., 1975.

Shaffer, D. H. "A Survey History of the American Spring Driven Clock 1840-1860." Supplement to *Bulletin of the NAWCC, Inc.* 9 (1973).

Slobin, Herman. *The Florence Kroeber Story.* Columbia, Pennsylvania: NAWCC, Inc., 1973.

Symonds, R. H. *Thomas Tompion: His Life and Work.* London: Spring Books, published 1951 by B. T. Botsford, Ltd., and in 1969 by The Hamlyn Publishing Group, Ltd.

Tyler, E. J. *Clocks & Watches.* New York: Golden Press, 1974.

Ullyett, Kenneth. *In Quest of Clocks.* London: The Hamlyn Publishing Group, Ltd., 1968.

Usher, Abbott Payson. *A History of Mechanical Inventions.* Cambridge, Massachusetts: Harvard University Press, 1954.

Willard, John Ware. *A History of Simon Willard Inventor and Clockmaker.* New York: Paul P. Appel, 1962.

Wood, Stacy B. C., Jr. "The Hoff Family: Master Clockmakers of Lancaster Borough." *Journal of the Lancaster Historical Society* LXXXI, 4, 1977.

_____. "Rudy Stoner 1728-1769, Early Lancaster Pennsylvania Clockmaker." *Journal of the Lancaster Historical Society* LXXX, 2, 1976.

_____ and Kramer, Stephen E., III. *Clockmakers of Lancaster County and Their Clocks 1750-1850.* New York: Van Nostrand Reinhold Company, 1977.

Index

Cardinal numerals (e.g., 137) indicate page numbers. Hyphenated numerals (e.g., 25-11) indicate numbered entries.

About the Author: Anita Schorsch, a well-known collector of American antiques, is a member of the National Association of Watch and Clock Collectors. A former commissioner of the Pennsylvania Historical and Museum Commission, she is the author of several books on the decorative arts.